WESTLAND ZERO ONE

WESTLAND ZERO ONE

— Colin Hague —

© Colin Hague, 2022

Published by Colin Hague

A CIP catalogue record for this book is available from the British Library.

ISBN 978-1-3999-3279-0

Book layout and cover design by Clare Brayshaw

Prepared and printed by:

York Publishing Services Ltd
64 Hallfield Road
Layerthorpe
York YO31 7ZQ

Tel: 01904 431213

Website: www.yps-publishing.co.uk

Contents

Foreword

The EH101 (now AW101) took centre stage in both Colin Hague's and my own career.

I joined Westland Helicopters in 1975 and was the Westland Chief Designer EH101 from 1981 to 1994. It was my privilege to work closely with Colin in his role as Westland Chief Test Pilot as he and his team developed and fine-tuned the EH101 into a helicopter whose handling qualities are respected and enjoyed by all her pilots.

Colin was well qualified for this role. His career in the Royal Navy commenced in 1962 flying Wessex 1 and Wasp before becoming ETPS test pilot at Boscombe Down in 1972. Here he had a leading role in testing Gazelle, Sea king and Lynx helicopters.

Joining Westland in 1979 at the start of the design phase he underpinned the design aim to endow the EH101 with unrivalled naval and small ship operating abilities. Becoming Chief Test Pilot in 1988 he led the flight development from first flight to entry into service. Having previously introduced the Lynx into naval use, including carrying out the first deck landings, he performed the same service for the EH101.

Not many people get to follow a major new aircraft from first definition to production, but Colin and I were fortunate enough to do so.

Enjoy the insights given in this important life story.

Brian Main MBE
Westland Chief Designer EH101 (1981–1994)

Introduction

Westland One is the jealously guarded radio call sign used solely by the Chief Test Pilot of Westland helicopter, and Westland Aircraft before that, going back to the days of Harold Penrose in the thirties. It was my privilege to use it for fifteen years, longer than any other recent occupant.

When I was guiding at the Fleet Air Arm Museum I was frequently asked if I had written a book about my career and experiences. I had never thought about it, or had the time, but when the Covid Pandemic broke out in March 2020 and we were all confined to our homes it seemed the ideal opportunity to get out my Log Book and start writing. Two and a half years of single finger typing were combined into a series of memoirs.

Encouraged and supported as always by my wife Mags, the memoirs slowly took shape. The Log Book entries often reminded me of specific events, but more often of periods of intense activity, particularly in the Cold War.

In modern times a test pilot is fortunate if he is involved in any new type at all. It has been my privilege to see the EH101/Merlin progress from ideas on paper to entry into service, and be successful worldwide.

I hope you enjoy reading about my journey through more than fifty years of aviation.

Colin Hague OBE FraeS

Acknowledgements

I would to thank the following for their help for this my first venture in to authorship;

My friend and colleague Brian Main.

Simon Pryor of Leonardo's for his help in finding the photographs.

Leonardo's for their permission to use them.

Clare and Cathi of YPS for their help and encouragement.

My wife Mags for her unfailing support.

CHAPTER 1

Early Days

I was born on 10th June 1944, four days after D-day, in Sheffield. On looking back it was very brave of my parents to expand their family with all the difficulties of wartime. My elder brother John was born in 1941 and my younger brother Jim came along in 1948. My father was a manager at a Spring firm in Sheffield, having joined as an office boy and worked his way up. I guess he was in a reserved occupation, as he was never called up. He was however, in the Home Guard where he reached the dizzy heights of Second Lieutenant! My mother was Scottish and worked hard at home with three boys, no washing machine and a very dirty Sheffield atmosphere.

I had a very happy childhood in a small semi-detached house in the suburbs of Sheffield. Money must have been tight but we never lacked for anything and we were taught that if you wanted anything you saved up your pocket money for it. We all went to the local Primary school, Greystones, which was within walking distance. It was a basic Yorkshire school which concentrated on the three

R's and passing the 11 plus exam. This dictated which secondary school you went to, the top ones going to the Grammar schools and then on to University. I must have passed OK, as I was awarded a Scholarship from a local trust, of £30, no small sum in those days. I had my eyes on a new Meccano set but it finally purchased a new overcoat. We had to go to Sheffield Town Hall to collect the money, which was a great adventure. Greystones was an excellent primary school and I was fortunate to start my education there. In my last year there I was Head Boy.

I had passed to go to King Edward VII Grammar school for boys, the top school in Sheffield. Going to a new school is always a difficult period but I was helped by the fact that my brother was already there. I had to get to grips with a whole range of new subjects, including French and Latin. Latin was mandatory, as at that time it was a mandatory requirement to get into Oxford or Cambridge, which was the main aim of the school. It was expected that everyone would go to University, anything else was second rate. For every ten people who got in to Oxbridge the school had a half day holiday.

Discipline was very strict and the cane was still in use and I was beaten twice for minor homework misdemeanours. It was very painful and I still had the stripes days later. I think some of the masters got a vicarious pleasure out of it. It is unthinkable these days.

The Headmaster Mr Clapton was a fearsome figure and we were all terrified of him. It was unthinkable to go to him for advice and a summons to his study was dreaded, though I had to do it as I was changing schools. My father had got a new job at another Spring firm at West Bromwich in the Midlands. This must have been another brave decision on his part, as he had spent all his working life with one firm in Sheffield. It meant moving the family to a new house in Sutton Coldfield and buying a house for the first time. I did not want to move, as it meant leaving all my friends but I had no choice. I was to start again at another Grammar school, Bishop Vesey's, at Sutton Coldfield.

I joined the Boy Scout movement while I was at King Edwards and this was to play a major part in my life for the next few years. There were three troops there and I joined C troop, who met on Saturday afternoons, with a very keen and enthusiastic Scoutmaster, Mr Johnson. The troop had two camps a year, for one week at Whit half term and one for two weeks in the summer. What a responsibility for the leaders, to take a bunch of teenage boys, who had to cook for themselves on an open wood fire. We had to find and chop the wood ourselves, with a hand axe and a felling axe, supervised by boys only two years older! It was miraculous there were no accidents. My first long camp was to the Brecon Beacons, which meant a long train journey, which must have been difficult in itself to organise. A separate lorry took all our heavy kit, tents, tools etc which must have been waiting for us at the remote farm. A highlight of that camp was a day trip by coach to the International Scout Jamboree in Sutton Park near Birmingham. Little did I know that in a few years time I would be living in a house next to the Park!

My second long camp was to Borrowdale in the Lake District, which we didn't know was actually the wettest place in England! It certainly lived up to its reputation while we were there. We travelled there by packing all the kit in a furniture van and all the scouts, for a five hour trip! No Health and Safety in those days.

I enjoyed my time in the Scouts and it certainly taught you self reliance, leadership and how to get on with people in difficult circumstances. I was chosen to read the Scout

Law at the annual St. Georges day parade in Sheffield City Hall, in front of thousands of other Scouts, my first occasion of public speaking.

While I was at King Edwards I had my first minor parts in school plays, one of which was Oedipus Rex, translated and published by our Latin master, Mr Watling, who I later found was a distinguished classical scholar. It was a privilege to be taught by him, although we didn't realise it at the time.

Just before I left school after four years, I was able to participate in a school trip to Sweden. This was a party of ten, lead by our English master, Mr Burns. The aim was to stay at a Boarding school at Grebbestad on the west coast to assist at an English course of Swedish boys, living with them at the school. It meant my first flight, in a Handley Page Hermes, which I found very exciting. I was allowed to visit the cockpit and saw for the first time the complexity of the instruments and controls. The visit, my first time abroad, was a great success and we all enjoyed the different food and the perfect weather. We returned on a rather ancient ferry from Gothenburg to Tilbury, my first time at sea.

Our family holidays from Sheffield were the same for many years, hiring a house at the small Welsh coastal village of Llangranog, for a fortnight. We always went with another family, the Oswalds, who had been neighbours in Sheffield. They had two boys the same age as myself and my elder brother and we were and have remained lifelong friends. Llangranog was the perfect place for family holidays, with two sandy beaches and beautiful countryside. The weather wasn't always perfect, so we always took lots of games and even model aircraft kits to make. It was a lovely holiday for us boys but catering for all those hungry mouths must have been a nightmare for the two mothers.

We also spent a lot of our holidays with my mother's Scottish relatives in a small town called Milngavie (pronounced Mulguy), just on the outskirts of Glasgow. My grandfather Watt owned and ran a smallholding and grain mill, which was still powered by a water wheel. This was fascinating for us of course and in our early days there were cows and chickens, looked after by my Aunt. Later on in my teens I would go and work with the delivery driver, my first paid job. He also let me drive the lorry but not on the roads. Unfortunately, the whole business was too small to survive and eventually closed down.

I had always been fascinated by aircraft and aviation, inspired by the aviation section in Meccano Magazine. I had always enjoyed building models in Meccano, which was a construction kit using metal plates and nuts and bolts, a very early introduction to engineering. I also started making the early plastic model kits and then moved on to flying model kits. These were produced by a firm called Keil Kraft, made of balsa wood and covered in tissue paper. The parts were printed on thin sheets of balsa wood and had to be cut out with a sharp modelling knife and then assembled with stringers, very similar to real aircraft construction as I was to find out later in life. The aircraft were powered by an elastic band, which was wound up and that drove the propeller. This was fine for propellor aircraft (Spitfire, Hurricane etc) but they also produced a range of jet aircraft (Hunter, Sabre etc) powered by a small 'jet' engine. This was called a Jetex engine and was a small tube with a nozzle at one end. Into this you put a small chemical pellet, ignited by a fuse. This got so hot the kit included an Asbestos patch to prevent the aircraft catching fire! The models never did fly very well and inevitably eventually crashed.

My elder brother was much more advanced and built flying models powered by small diesel engines. These were either free flying, which you hoped wouldn't go too far, or control line, where the aircraft was controlled by two wires, attached to a handle, held by an operator in the middle of the circle as the aircraft went round and round. He financed these by an early morning paper round. I was never as ambitious as him and acted as his assistant. The only time I tried the control line model it crashed in the first few seconds and I burst into tears! John was so keen he even founded and ran a model aircraft club at school, which was a major achievement at such a conservative academy. However my interest in aviation had been kindled.

My new school in Sutton Coldfield had a different approach to exams than my school in Sheffield where it was expected that all of the top three sets would take O-levels after four years and A-levels after six. At Sutton it was the other way round, only the top set did this, as I had done, so I was joining straight into the sixth form, without knowing what my choices were until my first day in my new school. This choice of course dictated what A-levels I should do and what I should study at University, a major turning point in life, although I didn't realise it at the time. In the short time I had to choose I chose Geography, French and Maths, as they were subjects I liked. I had no thought of future planning at all! I had no wish to follow the Sciences or the Arts, so it was the start of a lifelong interest in Geography, helped by a young and enthusiastic Physical Geography teacher, John Howell, whom we shall meet again later.

Another feature of the new school was a large and enthusiastic Scout Group, lead by the Headmaster himself, Geoff Cross, who was a very different character to the man in Sheffield. As I was 15 I joined the Senior Scout section, lead by the previously mentioned John Howell. This tended to do more adventurous activities and helped with the junior troops. My younger brother Jim, who was 11, joined the school at the same time as I did and the Scouts as well.

Our Senior Scout summer camp was very ambitious, a two week hiking trip to the Scottish Highlands, carrying all our equipment, tents, sleeping bag, cooking equipment etc. Fortunately, the weather was very kind to us and we even had one night camping on the summit of Ben More, the highest mountain in the area. We cooked on Primus stoves, very primitive paraffin cookers, lightweight but very effective. Once again we were lead by John Howell, who seemed very old to us but was probably in his late twenties!

We were also expected to help with running the Junior Scout groups, which was very good experience for us, including going to their Summer camp in Wales. One year there was an outbreak of sickness, probably caused by dirty water and we Seniors spent most of our time as nurses. My youngest brother was one of those affected, so I was busy doing all his washing as well.

The school owned a cottage in Snowdonia, which we used for adventure training, hiking and rock climbing. There was a flourishing Mountaineering Club at the school of which I was a keen member. I spent several weekends hiking in Wales, or rock climbing in Derbyshire. One of the aims of the club was to have a team complete the Fourteen Peaks hike in Snowdonia. This involved climbing all those mountains in Snowdonia which were over 3000ft in height, non-stop. This meant starting off in darkness from the top of Snowdon, which was an adventure in itself. The weather had to be ideal for this but nonetheless it was a terrific responsibility for the Masters involved, one of whom was John Howell. Despite a lot of training for this (cross country running in climbing boots), I didn't complete the whole route but just managed seven of them, including the summit of Snowdon in the dark.

On the Scouting front, I had decided to use the free time after A-levels to obtain the requirements for the Queen's Scout badge, the highest level in the movement. This was presented to me at the school, but it also meant I was entitled to take part in the annual Queen's Scouts parade past the Queen Mother at Windsor Castle, a great honour. I did this with a particular friend of mine from school, Keith Bromhead, who had changed to be a boarder at school, when his parents moved to Cheam. Before the Parade we had just spent several days camping and canoeing on the Thames on a canoe Keith had built himself. This had gone fine until we were caught downstream of an emptying lock and were pushed underneath an adjacent jetty. There was room for the canoe but not for us, so over we went! Fortunately we did not have all our kit on board and there were people around to help us. It was also a warm April day so we soon dried out.

Things hadn't been going too well scholastically and I had failed my first attempt at Maths A-level, passing French and Geography. These were not enough to go to Newcastle University to read Geography or Geology, so I had to repeat the year again, this time with a different Maths teacher, who would accept no failures! This time I passed and was accepted at the University but things had changed in my career path.

I mentioned before my interest in flying and I had decided to try and become a pilot rather than go to University. I had found out about the College for Air Training at Hamble in Hampshire. This was a two year course funded by BOAC and BEA to provide them with a source of newly qualified pilots. The entry requirements were very strict, with long interviews at Hamble and they had hundred of applicants. I also had to pass the very strict medical requirements of the CAA and the companies. Taking the CAA medical first in London I was very surprised to discover I was a little short sighted in one eye. It was just within limits for a Licence but when I did the repeat medical at Heathrow, BOAC failed me as they weren't prepared to take the risk. I was devastated, as I had never considered failure. Fortunately I had considered other aspects of flying and discovered one could join the Royal Navy as a helicopter pilot with a slight latitude in eyesight, so I promptly applied!

This lead to a series of interviews and assessments at the Admiralty Interview Board at Gosport, which followed a flying aptitude assessment at RAF Biggin Hill. These were similar to ones I had already been through at Hamble, which was an advantage. One of the leadership tests was to lead a team across a pond, using planks which were not quite long enough. I remembered a solution from an old Rupert book puzzle and sailed through it! The final interview was with the whole Board, which was very daunting. However, I must have passed, as shortly after I received a letter telling me that I had been accepted for a Short Service commission as a helicopter pilot in the Royal Navy. This arrived at about the same time as a letter of acceptance from Newcastle University! At this turning point in my life I decided I would enjoy a flying career rather than a scholastic one. As it turned out it was the right decision.

As it happened I found out much later in life that all the student pilots at the College in what would have been my entry all joined BEA and I would have spent my career flying short haul around Europe, not the exotic long haul I had imagined! I had seen the advertisements for helicopter pilots in various magazines but I must confess I would never have considered them if I hadn't been rejected elsewhere.

I decided on a Short Service commission as that gave me the option to leave after 5, 8 or 10 years or to retire at the age of 38. I was not interested, at that time, in a permanent commission which would have lead to driving ships and trying to achieve higher rank. The navy dropped the five year options shortly after I joined as too many pilots were leaving after having trained and carried out just one front line tour. At that time the Fleet Air Arm was expanding and there was a shortage of aircrew, so the Short Service commissions were introduced. The Navy had five Aircraft Carriers in commission when I joined!

CHAPTER 2

Dartmouth and Flying Training

All Naval Officers go to the Britannia Royal Naval College for their initial training, as they are all Officers first, whatever their specialisation. When I joined in 1962, General list (full career) cadets did two years there, including some time at sea, while Supplementray list (Short service commission) did two terms. We were all combined together for the first six weeks of Basic Training, which like all military training was made very physical and tiring.

Most of us had no idea what was waiting for us when we got off the train at Kingswear to catch the ferry across the River Dart to the Dartmouth side on September 15th 1962. We were formed up into a large group and marched up the hill towards the very imposing frontage of the College. There was a particularly large entry that year, around 300 and we were divided into Divisions. This was rather like the House system at school and was used for sports and administration. The Divisions were named after Naval heroes and I entered Blake Junior Division. I was allocated a bed space in a room (or Cabin in naval speak) with seven other cadets, all of whom were Supplementary list aircrew.

We slept in double bunks and had a wardrobe each in which the clothes had to be placed in a very specific order which we very rapidly learnt.

The first six weeks were very physical, with a lot of physical training, swimming and Parade Training. These activities all started at 0630 so it was a very early start every day. We also had to look after the vast amount of uniform we had been given, including the boots, which had to be transformed from brand new dull black to an immaculate mirror finish. There was no leave allowed for the first six weeks but everyone was so tired there was little wish to go out. Living in an eight bed cabin with seven others in close proximity for three months was undoubtedly to give us a taste of living in a Messdeck. You made friends very quickly and learned to get on with others who may not have been a friend. Most of us had joined straight from school, so had no experience of being away from home, or communal living. The one exception was Raymond Matthews (Mat) who was an ex rating and was a few years older, who was making the difficult transition from junior rating to Officer training.

Having been through basic training himself he was an invaluable source of information for the rest of us. To start with he must have thought us very juvenile but in the frantic pace of life in the first six weeks we soon gelled together. We were occupied doing something from 0600 to 2100, with only short breaks for meals and we were chased and harried by a group of Senior Rating Instructors. They were the Physical Trainers, Parade Training Instructors and Seamanship Instructors, all of whom specially selected as the best in their branch.

Sports and boat work played a major part in our activity. There were several types of boats we had to pass a competency test in. This was particularly interesting for me as I had very little previous experience of boats, either sailing or powered. At the end of my two terms at Dartmouth I had qualified on all seven varieties, from two man sailing dinghies to 40 foot two engine Picket boats. I enjoyed them all and the dinghy sailing I was able to continue in my time in the Navy. On the sporting side I learnt to play Squash, a game I knew nothing about. I continued to play for many years, both in the Navy and later. My initial teacher at Dartmouth was another Cadet, Robin Bawtree, whom I later found out was the Naval champion for many years. By a strange coincidence we became near neighbours after we had left the Navy.

All the boat work was carried out on the River Dart, whatever the weather. The boats were all moored at the College's jetty at Sandquay, which was at sea level. The College was a great deal higher up the hill and there was a very long series of steps between the two. Going down was no problem but it was a long tiring climb back again!

I particularly enjoyed qualifying on the two large sailing boats, a 27 ft Whaler, which was the Naval standard sea boat in use at the time and the 35 ft Cutter, which hadn't changed much since Nelson's time. The cutter could be sailed or rowed and was used for early morning pulling, with crews of 10 or more. That really woke you up at 0700 on a dark freezing morning!

I haven't mentioned the weather during my stay at Dartmouth during the winter of 1962/3 but it was the coldest in living memory. There were piles of snow around the Parade ground when we came back from Christmas leave which were still there at Easter. The weather wasn't allowed to stop many activities and we were out sailing in the Whaler when a sudden gust of wind caused it to capsize and tip the crew of seven into the freezing river Dart. Fortunately we were all wearing life jackets but we were also wearing several layers of clothes and oilskins, which rapidly became sodden. It seemed to take an age before we were picked up and we had great difficulty climbing back up the ladders onto the rescue boats as we were so heavy. We then had to run back up the steps to the warm baths and showers in the College.

After the initial six weeks we were then split up into groups which more reflected the specialisation, so I was now in a class of 20 prospective aircrew and the course became more academic and less physical, though we still had early morning activities. I particularly enjoyed the Naval History lectures, which covered the whole period from Nelson to World War II.

All the Aircrew cadets who aspired to be pilots had to go through a grading assessment on the College Tiger Moth fleet. These old bi-plane trainers were kept at Roborough airfield on the outskirts of Plymouth and were flown by a group of long retired ex-service aviators as instructors. It was planned that we flew 10 hours in the three weeks allocated, at the end of which we may have got to solo standard. My class's flying period happened to be in November, so with the open cockpit we were very cold. We thus wore as much clothing as possible, looking more like the Michelin Man than aspiring pilots. Although we were pleased and thrilled to be airborne, it was not a good time to be a student pilot as we were freezing cold and also had poor communications with the Instructor. The Tiger Moth had a very basic intercom system, which ran off a 12 volt battery system, as the aircraft had no electrical system. I could hardly hear what my Instructor was saying but was too nervous to say so and thus did not make great progress. I flew a total of 12 hours there in a series of short flights but did not go solo, along with the majority of my fellow students. There is a much more severe grading system now and I am sure I would have been failed at that stage. Fortunately I wasn't and went on to go solo later in a reasonable time once I had proper instructions which I could hear!

My family had never been particularly religious but had a background of Scottish Presbyterianism. I had never been confirmed so thought it was a good thing to do at Dartmouth, being strongly encouraged by the Free Churches padre there, the Rev John Goudie, who made a very strong impression on me. After a period of instruction I was confirmed in the small Chapel of Dartmouth, by the Senior Naval Chaplain. My parents made the long journey down from the Midlands for this, which was their first encounter with the Navy and they were much impressed, especially when they were invited into drinks with the Captain. They were very nervous to start with but he soon put them at ease.

After Christmas leave we returned to find all eight of us from room 166 were now sharing a large dormitory with another thirty cadets, still on the same bunk beds. We had even less privacy now but were allocated some smaller room to study. The routine was just as vigorous but seemed easier as we were more used to it. The whole dormitory was for the short service cadets, the general list cadets still had rooms of their own, which did cause some jealousy!

Of the original eight of us from Cabin 166 only two of us were helicopter pilots, the others were fixed wing pilots or Observers. My helicopter colleague was John Habgood, who like me had a slight eyesight defect. We were to become firm friends during flying training and on our first

Squadron. Of the others, two qualified as Observers, one qualified as a Gannet pilot and two failed pilot training and left. Mat whom I previously mentioned failed pilot training but was offered Observer training, which he accepted. He qualified on Sea Vixens but unfortunately was killed in a deck landing accident on his first tour. The casualty list on Vixens was very high, particularly on the smaller Carriers.

During the second term at Dartmouth all the Naval Air Cadets had to spend two weeks on board HMS Brearley, an old Inshore Minesweeper. This was to show us the life at sea from the sailors point of view, as we were acting as them. One week was spent in harbour, carrying out maintenance (painting etc), and five days were spent at sea, on a short voyage from Dartmouth to Portsmouth, with a stop at Poole. Although the sea wasn't rough, a lot of people were seasick. I was fortunate as my job was helmsman, using the wheel on the bridge in the open air, so I wasn't too badly affected. My relief never turned up, so I had a long spell which suited me. As we cadets were doing the cooking, with some guidance from the permanent staff, the food was of variable quality, but we all survived.

As we were passing through the Portland exercise areas a Wessex 1 came and hovered close by which was my first introduction to this aircraft which was going to play a major part in my life later in my career. There was one helicopter attached to the College, an old Dragonfly, which at this time was coming to the end of its time in the Navy, giving experience flights to Cadets. The Dragonfly was the first helicopter in Naval service which had a proper role, Search and Rescue ashore, and Planeguard on the Carriers. So I had my first helicopter time in the Navy's first proper helicopter. The pilot was Lt. Larry Hallett, who many years later I was to meet again when I was working in the Fleet

Air Arm Museum, where they had the last Naval Dragonfly on display.

As we drew nearer to the end of my two terms at Dartmouth we started to have final exams and assessments of the non academic activities. To my delight and surprise I finished with a first class pass, being third out of a class of forty eight. This also meant six months increase in seniority, a big financial benefit later on.

There was of course a passing out parade which my parents and brothers attended, and I was now promoted to Midshipman.

Because the training pipeline could only accommodate a certain number of students, the class was split in to two, the first half departing to initial flying training immediately after Easter leave. The second half was held over for about three months, on a series of courses to fill the time in. These consisted of two weeks with the Royal Marines at Lympstone in Devon, two weeks at HMS Condor, the engineering training school at Arbroath, and two weeks of survival training at Seafield Park in Gosport.

The two weeks at Lympstone were deliberately very hard, almost like a Marine initial course, with speed marches, obstacle course and weapon firing.

The Young Marine Officers course (YO's) was also running at Lympstone, and one of our number put up a recruiting advertisement for the Fleet Air Arm, implying it was not too late for them to join! This of course infuriated them, and that night a number of us Air cadets were "kidnapped" by the YO's, and still in their pyjamas, were dropped off at various points in the local countryside! This of course soon came to the attention of the local police and press, and lead to a big inquiry next morning. Fortunately we were off on an exercise on Dartmoor for two days, so by the time we came back it had all blown over. I think the YO's all had their leave stopped for a fortnight.

After a lengthy train journey from Exeter to Arbroath, on the east coast of Scotland, we joined HMS Condor, at that time the Engineering school for Apprentices. We did some hands on engineering on the aircraft there, but the highlight of the fortnight was a familiarisation flight in an old Sea Prince aircraft, which was based there to give the students some flying experience. It was cold, noisy and drafty, so it was not really too much of a treat. We also had a three day stay at the cottage belonging to Condor in the Highlands. This was at the base of Ben Nevis, which we all climbed. Fortunately the weather was very kind to us while we were there.

After another long train journey back down to Portsmouth we joined the substantial Mansion which was the Wardroom of the School of survival training at Seafield Park, which was part of the nearby Naval Air Station, HMS Ariel, which at that time was also the Headquarters of the Fleet Air Arm. The course consisted of a week's classroom instruction, followed by three days "surviving" in the New Forest. Fortunately for us we were doing the course in June, and the weather was very pleasant, as we had to build a shelter, and sleep in it. We had no food for the first two days, the idea being we should trap something. All the rabbits in the New Forest were far too clever to be caught, of course, so eventually we were given two dead rabbits, which in no time were skinned, gutted and on the fire. They tasted delicious! Having completed the course we then had to make our own way to RAF Linton-on-Ouse to start our flying training.

CHAPTER 3

Basic Flying Training

RAF Linton-on-Ouse was the home of No. 1 Flying Training School where all Naval aircrew carried out their basic training, the fixed wing pilots spending a year on Jet Provosts, or the very last of the Vampires. Helicopter pilots flew 80 hours on Chipmunks, which took about three months. The Chipmunk was a simple low wing trainer, with a tandem cockpit, the instructor sitting in the rear seat. I was part of No. 112 HSP course (Helicopter Specialist), which consisted of six Midshipmen, like myself, and two career sub-lieutenants.

The course started with a week's ground school given to us by a series of RAF Chief Technicians. The Chipmunks, being much slower than the jets, were based at nearby RAF Dishforth, so we were bussed over there on a daily basis, and did all our circuit flying there. My instructor was Flight Lieutenant Jerry Baxter, and I had my first flight with him on July 7th 1963. The Chipmunk was not a comfortable aircraft; you were sitting on a parachute pack, and had to wear an oxygen mask, not for oxygen but to use the built in intercom microphone. The mask, being new had a very strong rubber smell, which didn't help if you were prone to airsickness. Fortunately that never bothered me, and I started to enjoy the wonderful experience of being airborne, and learning the basics of flying straight and level and turns. The summer of 1963 was a beautiful one, with day after day of sunshine and light winds, perfect for us beginners. After the five hours of basic handling we started on the intensive circuit training. After about another five hours I was sent off solo on July 25th, an experience never to be forgotten. Once airborne the sudden realisation that there is no one in the rear seat, and it is all up to you! It is a great boost to one's confidence, and the next day I was sent off again, after a short check. Then followed an intensive period of about six hours of solo circuits and landings.

Once that has been satisfactorily completed, we moved on to General Handling, which was the introduction to Aerobatics, and practice forced landings. A lot of emphasis was placed on this, the correct selection of a field and then making a practice power off approach, only over shooting at the last minute. I really enjoyed aerobatics, looping, barrel rolls, slow rolls and spinning, enjoying the freedom of the skies.

Mean while the rest of the course was also progressing, they had all gone solo, and no one was "chopped", the dreaded word for failing the course, and being removed. This was not the case with our fixed wing colleagues, a number of whom had already left. That pressure is always at the back of one's mind during flying training, and it can be intense. One of our course, John Habgood, who was becoming a good friend, was not sent off solo when he was expecting it, and burst in to tears. He succeeded the next day, much to his relief.

Halfway through the course we had a progress check with a different more Senior instructor, before progressing to the next phase, Instrument flying. Instrument flying training was carried out by the student sitting in the rear cockpit, with the transparent cockpit obscured by a type of whitewash, so he has no eternal reference. I always enjoyed Instrument flying, and in fact went on to eventually become an examiner. Thirteen hours was spent on this phase of training, a fair proportion, with a test at the end.

Interspersed with this were our first Navigation exercises, around the local countryside, and our first opportunity to get lost! It was not too difficult to find Dishforth, as it was adjacent to the main York to Newcastle railway line, which was a major feature, provided you turned in the right direction.

We were also introduced to formation flying and night flying, the latter including a solo night circuit, and a night navigation exercise. There was then a heavy session of general handling (five sorties in one day) before the Final Handling Test. This was flown with the Deputy Chief Instructor, and was the final step to completing the course. I must have passed OK, as it turned out I was top of the course, though I didn't find that out till much later.

There wasn't much activity on the social side while we were at Linton, as we had very little money, and no transport, Linton being eleven mile from York, the nearest centre of entertainment. One of the ground instructors had a car for sale a BMW Isetta bubble car. This was a two seater powered by a 300cc motor cycle engine. Even at £50 it was more than I could afford, so I had the temerity to borrow the money from the bank, with my newly opened account at Lloyds! My first car didn't turn out to be the most reliable, although it never let me down. It needed a lot of expensive work on the engine, but it eventually got me and all my kit from Yorkshire to Cornwall, which is where I was bound for the next phase of training.

After a short spell of leave at home I set off for Cornwall in my little Bubble car, packed in with all my kit. It was a long way (300+miles), and it was the first time I had attempted it. Fortunately one of my course colleagues' parents lived near Bristol, about half way on the journey, and I was invited to spend the night there. We both set off for Culdrose next morning, Roger in his very old Lea-Francis which he had bought in Yorkshire, and which already had experienced several breakdowns!

❄

CHAPTER 4

Helicopter Training

R NAS Culdrose is situated at the tip of Cornwall on
the Lizard Peninsula. It is directly in the way of the
weather systems coming in from the Atlantic, and thus
has a rather poor weather factor, and is famous for its
"horizontal fogs". At that time it was the main base for all
Naval helicopters, and was to be my home, on and off for
the next four years. We were joining 705 Squadron, which
was the basic helicopter training unit. The first 50 hours
were flown on Hiller 12E's, a small but tough American
aircraft, with a single piston engine. The second 50 hours
were on Westland Whirlwinds. Mk.3 or7, a much bigger
aircraft with a cabin big enough for seven troops and at
that time (1964) still in operational use in the Commando
squadrons.

My instructor was Lieutenant Bill Berry with whom I
got on fairly well. After the inevitable ground school where
we learnt all about the aircraft, we started flying helicopters
in November 1963. The first few hours were making the
difficult transition to helicopters, initially learning to hover,
which at first seems quite impossible. Completely different

controls to a Chipmunk, and it was impossible to move one without having to make adjustments on the other two! I managed to go solo after9 hours, which was about average, and it was just as thrilling as the first Chipmunk solo.

Then followed another thirty hours of consolidation, twenty of which were solo, learning the peculiarities of helicopters, especially the autorotations to engine off landings. The Hiller was very forgiving in this respect, and was a great training introduction to helicopters.

As Culdrose at this time was still a fixed wing base most of the helicopter training flights took place at Predannack, a satellite airfield a few miles south, where we could fly our circuits and practice hovering undisturbed.

Having been checked out in Hillers we moved on to the Whirlwinds, which was a great step up. These were much bigger machines (7000 lbs), which the Navy originally purchased in the anti –submarine role, which involved long periods of hovering over the sea at high power, with the sonar body in the water. They were also used by the Commando squadrons, as I was to find out later in the year. There were two versions, the Mk. 3 with a seven cylinder 700HP Wright engine, which had an electric starter. The Mk. 7 had a fourteen cylinder 755HP Leonides engine, and a cartridge starting system. The Mk.3's were quite elderly and were gradually being replaced by the Mk. 7, which had a poor reliability record. At the time of our training the Mk 3 aircraft in 705 were the last in service. There was no difference in handling between the two types, so we happily swapped between them. There was no autopilot or cyclic trim on the Whirlwind, so the pilot has to hold the controls the whole time. The Mk. 7 had a cartridge starting system, with the "barrel" protruding from the nose the aircraft. The barrel was like a revolver, with spaces for six cartridges, but we were never allowed to have more than one in at any time. On a cold morning with a reluctant engine one could get through a number of cartridges! There was also a safety disc in the system which would blow if the engine was too stiff to turn. This could be replaced by a sixpenny piece in an emergency, with the risk of blowing up the starter!

I enjoyed the conversion to an operational aircraft, and went solo after about four hours. The flying consisted of general handling and an introduction to Instrument flying, and also our first introduction to winching. This was carried out in Carrick Roads, the large expanse of water just off Falmouth. A very brave Aircrewman came with us for this, bearing in mind our very low levels of experience. The exercise was to recover a float we had previously dropped, using a grapnel attached to the winch hook. The final exercise was lowering the Aircrewman on the winch, conning us through a very long lead attached to the aircraft's intercom system. Bearing in mind there was no one else in the cabin to help, it showed a great degree of trust, and we were learning the teamwork which must exist between aircrew which is vital for this.

After I had flown about fifteen hours on Whirlwinds I was involved in an incident which almost brought my career to an abrupt halt. I was sent off solo to practice sloping ground landings in a special area of the airfield which happened to be downwind of the Squadron dispersal I was starting from. This meant taking off, flying a short distance into wind, and then a 180 degree turn downwind, then a decelerating turn back in to wind, a manoeuvre known as a downwind fast stop which I had just learnt how to do. There was a strong, gusty wind that day and I misjudged the power needed in the final turn, and started to descend. I hit the ground with two of the four undercarriage legs, and fortunately bounced back upright as I struggled to regain control. The controller in ATC had noticed my difficulty (his finger was poised on the crash button) and had informed the squadron, who ordered me to return. My instructor came out of the aircraft, saw how upset I was, and immediately took me off for a general handling sortie, including several downwind fast stops. I realise now he did it to regain my confidence for which I will always be grateful. Inspecting the aircraft on our return a small crack was noticed on the bulkhead to which was attached one of the front under carriage legs.

I had to fill in the Form A25, the accident reporting form, for the first time, and I was convinced I was about to be chopped. However, after a long debrief I carried on with the rest of the course. On my final handling check with the Squadron CO I almost did it again, and a severe warning notice was incorporated into my records, and for the rest of my career I was always nervous of that particular manoeuvre.

Our basic training was now complete; the next phase was operational training, so we had to decide which arm we wanted, Anti-submarine or Commando. As we were aware of the action in the Far East involving the Commando Squadrons most of us wished to go that way, including me! I don't know how the selection was made, but I was very pleased when I was chosen to go that way. At this point we were awarded our Wings at a special ceremony, to which my parents came down. . This was a major point in our training, and we were very proud of the wings on our sleeves, especially as we were still Midshipmen.

The Commando operational training Squadron was 847, still using Whirlwinds Mk. 7. We were of course familiar with these from 705, but now we were going to learn how to use them. Our instructors were now not Qualified Helicopter Instructors, but ex- operational pilots. The flying was all to train us in operational techniques; underslung load lifts, formation, tactical low level flying, troop drills, winching and more instrument flying. It was all very exciting, and much more interesting than our basic course on 705. We also acted as "soldiers", carrying out troop drills in and out of the cabin, being winched and helping with the load lifting attachment. We did a lot of solo navigation exercises, leading on to Pinex's, which required you to find an actual exact position, simulating a patrol pick up. Much of the flying was low level, which we had not been permitted to do before.

One of the more advanced exercises was carrying out troop drills with real soldiers in the Salisbury plain exercise areas, and staying there overnight, with a formation of three aircraft. Having completed all that the return trip to Culdrose was planned, straight back into a strong headwind and deteriorating weather (a Culdrose speciality!). When it became obvious we weren't going to make it an airborne decision was made to divert to Dartmouth. As mentioned before there was a Dragonfly based there and a small landing ground. They were very surprised to receive a formation of Whirlwinds for an overnight stay. Being Midshipmen we were now allowed to drink in the Gunroom, which had been forbidden to us when we had been cadets at the College, barely a year before. We noticed many a covetous look at the wings on our sleeves! The next day, the weather having improved we made it back to Culdrose.

I also carried out the longest solo land away Navex, to RAF Chivenor in Devon, at that time a training airfield for Hunters. We also carried out my first deck landings, on HMS Lofoten. Lofoten was an old converted Tank Landing

Ship, which had the well deck covered over to provide a deck specifically for helicopter landing practice. Being flat bottomed it rolled a lot, which was excellent practice for us. After four dual landings I was sent off solo for another seven. Little did I realise this was the beginning of a long association for me with deck operations, finishing my career with over 4000 landings. During night flying we also carried out flare drops for the first time.

Another demanding exercise was landing in a confined area. This was particularly important in jungle flying, which was where we were heading. We practised them in a small clearing in woods near St. Ives which when you first saw it from above looked ridiculously small. However we all managed several landings there and nobody clipped the trees.

As well as all the flying we had a lot of ground school on military subjects including three weeks at Old Sarum, near Salisbury, which was the Joint Operations centre, combining input from all three services. Old Sarum had a very old fashioned Army Mess, extremely comfortable with excellent food and service. There was also a croquet lawn, which we all learned while we were there! It was a shock for us to go back to our much more limited facilities at Culdrose.

I had decided my Bubble car was a bit small for long journeys, and sold it to a fellow officer on 847. My elder brother had some time before purchased an old Triumph Roadster, a convertible three seater with two "dickey seats" in the boot. This was a great fun car to have, but being old was expensive to run, so he offered it to me for £65! It was a much more comfortable trip back to Culdrose this time. It served me very well, and never let me down, except for a puncture and running out of fuel. The latter occasion was deeply embarrassing. I had invited a local girl to the Summer Ball and was running her home at midnight when we stopped about two miles short, out of petrol. It was a typical Cornish evening, heavy drizzle. I knew my friend Roger would also be coming along the road shortly, so we went to wait by the road. After a while when nothing happened and we were getting wet, I bravely stopped the first car that came along and explained the situation, and asked if they would at least take the girl home. The couple had just driven down from London and the man was most reluctant to help, but the lady was more sympathetic seeing us standing there still in our Ball outfits! They dropped the girl off home, and then dropped me off back on the main road, still six miles from Culdrose! I started to walk, determined to stop the first car that appeared. After about half an hour a car came along driven by my friend Roger. He kindly stopped to give me a lift, and was in fits of laughter all the way back. I rang and apologised to the girl next day, but understandably she wasn't too keen to see me again.

The Commando operational training lasted four months, about 100 hours flying, much of it solo, and did much to boost my confidence. We were ready to move on to the next and last part of our training, the conversion to Wessex Mk.1, at that time front line aircraft with 845 Squadron in the Far East. The Wessex was much bigger and more sophisticated aircraft than the Whirlwind. It was powered by a single large turbine engine, the Gazelle. This was one of the first matching of a turbine engine to a helicopter, and there had been many problems in development. The engine being large and heavy needed a powerful starting system, and this was provided by the ignition of a monofuel in a chamber. The ignition was provided by a large cartridge. A Monofuel is liquid which will burn without the need for oxygen. It is thus very volatile, and must be treated very carefully. If any air is left in the system after refuelling it tended to explode and blow out the side of the aircraft.

The Wessex 1 was one of the first helicopters to be provided with an Autopilot system, so for the first time we could safely let go the controls. The Wessex was first bought for the Royal Navy for Anti-submarine work, which involved hovering over the sea at 40 feet, and lowering a sonar transmitter. This had to be done day or night so the autopilot brought the aircraft automatically in to the hover, and maintained it using the sonar cable as the reference. These modes were more advanced than the ordinary flying, and the basic autopilot would maintain attitude and height, once engaged by the pilot. For this conversion to the Commando role we only used the basic autopilot, the mysteries of the advanced modes were reserved for yet another conversion later on.

The conversion was mainly getting used to a larger more sophisticated aircraft, and more instrument flying, at the end of which I was awarded my first Instrument rating, the White standard. Sometime in this period I was promoted to Act/Sub-Lieutenant, which is where the seniority I gained at Dartmouth came in to play, as I was now receiving higher pay.

During all our flying training I was particularly friendly with another student, John Habgood. We shared a room at Culdrose so we shared the stresses and difficulties and qualified together. We were both pleased when we found out we were both being sent to 845 Squadron in the Far East for our first operational tour. The Navy had two Commando squadrons at this time, 845 which we were joining and 848 who were reforming at Culdrose with new Wessex Mk 5. The two squadrons alternated with each other in the Far East about every two years. So we were on our way out east to our first proper job!

CHAPTER 5

845 Squadron

In 1964 it was a long and tortuous route out to Hong Kong where I was joining HMS Bulwark, which was the base ship for 845. RAF Transport Command had a regular route out to Singapore using Comet aircraft, stopping at El Adem in Libya, Aden, Gan and Singapore, about 24 hours in total. We departed from Lyneham in Wiltshire, the RAF terminal in UK. My father drove me down from home, where I had been on leave, and after an overnight stay we departed next morning. The Comet was very comfortable with rearward facing seats, and plenty of legroom. This was my first trip in a modern jet and I was very impressed, although the RAF food was very ordinary. We only stopped for a few hours at each refuelling stop. They were all very warm after the English Winter, but Gan left a distinct impression. It is an isolated coral atoll in the Indian Ocean which was a British possession, with an airfield built on it in World War 2, as a staging post. The heat and humidity hit you as soon as the aircraft door was opened, and although it was 3am there, a large crowd was assembled to view the passengers, particularly the female ones! Many years later I made a similar flight in a modern 747 nonstop 11hours!

We finally landed at RAF Changi on Singapore, which was one of four RAF airfields on the island. It turned out that Bulwark was in Hong Kong, so I had a few days to wait at the huge Naval base in Singapore, HMS Terror. This gave me a chance to get over the jet lag, and start to get used to the climate, which in Singapore was very hot (30 degrees+) and humid. The base had a very comfortable Officer's Club, with its own swimming pool, with which I was to become very familiar in the next few months.

I had a seat booked on chartered aircraft with British Eagle from Singapore to Hong Kong. This was on a Britannia which I shared with a company of Gurkhas going back to their base there. There was transport to take me to the ferry to Hong Kong Island on which was the Naval base and dockyard, where Bulwark was alongside.

This was my first time on a large ship, and it took a while to find my way around. I knew some of the other pilots who had been on the course previous to us, but most of the other pilots had been with the squadron some time and had a lot of experience flying in Borneo. The squadron was split in half, with half permanently ashore and the other half on the ship, participating in exercises or operations in Malaysia. The ship spent much of its time ferrying between Singapore and the Borneo coast.

The main reason for the operations ashore was supporting the army units in what became known as the Confrontation. After achieving in dependence in 1957 President Sukarno of adjoining Indonesia saw his opportunity to spread his Communist rule in to Malaysia with a series if incursions. The British military still having a large presence in the area acted to help the then very small and inexperienced Malaysian forces both in Malaysia and Borneo. Borneo was a very mountainous island, covered in thick primary jungle, split by very large rivers. The only way to get around was by boat, or helicopter. The RAF had very few helicopters so the Navy which had Commando Carriers with Royal Marines embarked and a squadron of helicopters were sent ashore to help. This became a lengthy campaign of about three years, and I arrived there about two years in.

As I was brand new I joined the part of the squadron on the ship and started off with more deck landings, Bulwark having a large flight deck, as it was an ex-fixed wing carrier. It was of course much bigger than Lofoten so the landings were much easier. Having been checked out by the CO, Lt. Cdr. "Tank" Sherman, I was sent off solo. Then followed a period of consolidation when I normally flew with a more experienced pilot. My first solo operational exercise was the withdrawal of a Royal Marine Commando from Labuan back to Bulwark, for transit back to Singapore, a role the ship was built for. The Commandos were specialists in Amphibious warfare and the Commando squadrons provide the lifting capacity from the ship to shore, the initial wave with troops and then the support with underslung loads, and sometimes vehicles and artillery.

I was also introduced to machine gun firing, the Wessex having the capability of two fixed forward firing machine guns. They were very much "scatter weapons", the sighting arrangements being a simple "ring and bead" sight, very similar to those used in World War 1. It was much easier to fit tracer bullets and for the pilot to "walk" the tracer on to the target, usually a splash target towed behind the ship. It was difficult to imagine when these guns might be used as the aircraft firing them would be very vulnerable to any fire returned from the ground.

I joined the ship in November 1964, and the ship was back in Hong Kong for Christmas, my first away from home. This was long before it became a tourist spot, and it was a very busy commercial port on the edge of Communist China, and was a very valuable trade outlet for them. The ex-patriot community was very glad to see the Navy there, and were very generous with their hospitality. Myself and two others were invited to a very lavish Christmas dinner by a retired English couple at their flat, which in some ways made up for not being at home.

After Christmas the ship sailed for Singapore, with a short visit to the huge American Naval base in the Philippines. In Singapore the Squadron disembarked to a small airfield at Sembawang, and prepared for the first exercise of the year, Exercise March Hare. This was to be an amphibious landing on the east coast of Malaya using the small airfield at Mersing as the landing point. The main difference in using an existing landing spot was that this was to take place at night, the first time this had been attempted! The Squadron did not do a lot of night flying so there was much night flying practice in February. As the first assault was usually a formation of three or four aircraft (to get as many troops on the ground as quickly as possible) it was decided to try the same at night. It soon proved to be too difficult as we could not see sufficient references to maintain a safe position, even by the very experienced pilots, After several scares it was decided to have a stream of aircraft rather than a formation, which we were very relieved about.

Years later night formation became possible with the right aids, mainly Night Vision Goggles, but they were way in the future for us.

All the night flying was with two pilots and I found myself tied up with the Squadron Senior Pilot, Lt. Cdr Brian Sarginson. Whether this was to help me get more experience or to help him with a younger pair if eyes I never discovered, but we seemed to get on OK. The exercise took place over four days and three nights without any incident, but it proved it would be very difficult to do it for real. After the exercise we were recalled to Singapore to help deal with a real operation which had built up while we were away.

In an attempt to persuade the local population to join them Indonesia had carried out a seaborne invasion of soldiers on the state of Johore, north of Singapore. Needless to say they had little success, and a Battalion of Ghurkhas and the newly formed Royal Malaysian Regiment were sent to round them up. For this they needed helicopter support, so we flew ashore immediately, firstly to Sembawang, where we were based, and then to RAF Seletar, which was the base for Operation Oaktree. Seletar was the base for a Squadron of RAF Whirlwind 10's, who would normally provide support for the military in the area. The Whirlwind was much smaller than our Wessex and the RAF seemed strangely reluctant to be available at weekends, so we had to cover for them! For about a week we did a lot of flying, lifting troops, supplies and ammunition for the troops working in the primary jungle. Needless to say the incursion was not a success, the local people did not rise up to join them, and the troops were soon rounded up.

One moment of excitement for us was when the aircraft we were flying developed a severe vibration, which is something you can never ignore in helicopters. The nearest place to land was a large clearing in the jungle, which unfortunately was in the area where the Indonesians might be! I was very pleased we had a troop of soldiers in the back who quickly fanned out round the aircraft to protect it. I even got my own Sterling machine gun out, which we always carried, although I doubt whether it would have been much use. A rescue party arrived who checked out the aircraft, who found nothing immediately wrong, and cleared the aircraft fit for one flight back to Sembawang for further investigation.

Operation Oaktree having been satisfactorily concluded we re-embarked on Bulwark and set off once more to the Borneo coast where I was to disembark for my eagerly awaited spell operating ashore.

845's operations were split into two. The main base was at the airfield at Sibu, a city on the large Rajang river about 80 miles inland from the coast. The other half of the detachment was at the forward operating base at Nanga Gat, a small community about 100 miles up the River Rajang. The four aircraft based there supported the operations close to the Indonesian border, about 80 miles away. This was where most of the action took place, with small four man patrols, which were inserted and recovered from small holes in the jungle by our aircraft. The Squadron had been operating from here for some time and was well accepted and welcomed by the local population.

Before my arrival there had been several accidents and some aircraft had been lost, fortunately with no fatalities. Some had been mechanical failures, but some were the result of operating an aircraft that had been designed to operate at sea level in the North Atlantic at high altitudes and temperatures, where the power was severely limited.

The pilot had little margin for error, frequently using full power to achieve a minimal vertical rate of climb coming out of clearings fully laden. With the Squadron split in two there were regular changes of aircrew between Sibu and Nanga Gaat. For my period ashore I was going to stay at Sibu and fly from there. As well as the Wessex there were two old Whirlwind 7's there, a hangover from the first naval squadrons ashore there several years before. They were useful for the shorter or less heavily loaded trips, frequently in medical support of the local population. As well as the military support an equally important role was winning the "hearts and minds" of the locals. This was achieved by frequently flying seriously ill patients from their widely scattered long houses to the main hospital in Sibu, thus avoiding a long boat trip. The patients were often women having difficulty in childbirth.

Shortly after I arrived at Sibu I was asked if I would like to fly the Whirlwind, as not all pilots kept in practice on it. Realising this meant the possibility of more flying (it was operationally quiet in the Sibu area) I readily volunteered. I was very familiar with the aircraft as I had just finished training on it some months before. It was only later on I realised most of the married men were not keen to fly it! However I enjoyed flying it and was involved in several medical flights to places I would never have visited. It only nearly let me down once, which I will describe later.

I arrived at Sibu at the beginning of April 1965 and spent the next three months there. I flew several ferry trips to Nanga Gaat but was never based there. I flew many casevac flights to Sibu, often with heavily pregnant women. We never had any actual births in the aircraft, but it came pretty close!

I had only been at Sibu about a week when a series of accidents resulted in the loss of three aircraft and several aircrew. The first was the loss of a Hiller, of which the squadron had two. They were used to transport small numbers of personnel to the very difficult sites at high altitude, where the performance of the Hiller was better than the Wessex. On landing on the small temporary wooden platform the aircraft slipped back and damaged the tail rotor. The pilot, John Morgan, was now in a quandary. The site was too high for a Wessex to hover and winch down personnel and spares, and the platform was blocked by the disabled Hiller. He decided to carry out temporary repairs on the tail rotor and attempt a short flight to a nearby site at a lower altitude. However shortly after lifting off the tail rotor failed, the aircraft crashed in to primary jungle and the pilot was killed.

The second accident was an airborne collision of two aircraft as they were returning to Nanga Gat. The two rotors touched and both aircraft crashed in the river which was in full flood at the time. Eleven people died in the accident, including my good friend John Habgood. None of the bodies or the airframes were ever recovered. Miraculously there was one survivor, the aircrewman who was slung out of the aircraft in to the river.

Shortly after that another good friend crashed at Nanga Gat when lifting out of a clearing not knowing he was overweight with a wrongly marked load. This was an example of how small the power margins were in the Wessex 1 in Borneo. Another Wessex had crashed before I went ashore, so the squadron lost five aircraft in a period of months. This obviously caused some disquiet back in Singapore and a number of Boards of enquiry had been set up, who all needed an officer to administer them. By this time I had been appointed as Staff Officer at Sibu, due to the rapid personnel changeover following the accidents, so I got the job.

As a very junior Sub-Lieutenant I would never normally be the Squadron Staff Officer. This job included dealing with all the CO's paperwork, acting as his PA, and most important, be responsible for paying all the sailors. This meant a weekly trip to Sibu's only bank to draw out large amounts of cash. Fortunately the Navy realised the possible difficulties of this, and I had a very experienced Supply Chief Petty Officer to help, who made sure everything was OK, and proper accounts were kept.

Accommodation for us officers was a new block of flats near the airport which was very comfortable. The Airport Manager's bungalow became the Wardroom where we took all our meals, cooked and served by three Chinese cooks and stewards brought ashore from Bulwark, so the food was excellent.

June 10th 1965 was my 21st birthday, which was of course a normal working day. Much to my surprise an English couple organised a surprise party for me at their house near the airport. He was an officer in the Royal Engineers topographical section, with whom we had a very close working relationship. He was on a long term stay in Sibu, so he had brought his wife and young family out there to live. It was extremely kind of them to go to so much trouble, and I know my parents were forever grateful.

As I mentioned I had offered to fly the Whirlwind, and so had several casevac trips bringing natives back to the hospital in Sibu. On one of the training flights with my friend Roger Bryant, I noticed one of the hydraulic pressures fluctuating. The Whirlwind has two independent systems for the controls, as the control forces would be too strong for the pilot without them. Although in theory you can carry on with one system I thought it prudent to land to investigate, as there was a village nearby with a football field. On landing looking at the fluid level in the reservoirs I was expecting to find one empty and one full. I was astonished to find both of them empty, with no obvious leaking hydraulic fluid beneath the aircraft. The systems are of course supposed to be entirely independent of each other, as a double hydraulic failure would be catastrophic. When the rescue team arrived they found a leak from the changeover valve, which is the one common point of the two systems. The leak was directly over the engine cooling fan, so the fluid was instantly evaporated. After repairs we made a cautious return back to Sibu. If we had not landed I am sure we would have very soon have lost control and crashed. It was a very narrow escape.

After three very busy months ashore at Sibu our relief Squadron , 848 arrived with their brand new Wessex 5's. These were twin engine aircraft, much more powerful than our Wessex 1's, and much more suitable for operations in Borneo. After a month's turnover at Sibu and Nanga Gaat, 845 finally left Borneo on June 30th 1965, and re-embarked as a complete squadron on Bulwark. The ship was heading for home, via a visit to Fremantle and a final exercise in Aden.

The visit to Fremantle was a huge success, and the ship was made very welcome, as always in Australia. During the long transit across the Indian Ocean there was little opportunity for flying, except for a trip to Gan to pick up mail, we arrived off Aden at the beginning of August 1965. The main purpose of the visit was to take part in an amphibious Exercise "Mixed Crop", further up the coast to the east of Aden, with a unit of Royal Marines and the loan of an RAF Wessex Mk. 2 from Khormaksar, the RAF's base at Aden. The Mk.2 was the same as the RN Mk.5 with two engines and was much more powerful than our Mk. 1's, especially in the high temperatures of the desert. The Marines were based at a small airfield about ten miles to the west of Aden called Falaise, and part of the squadron disembarked there to retrain the marines on helicopter drills. After a week of this we re-embarked again, with the Marines and set off for the exercise area.

The dawn assault soon showed the landing area was covered in a very fine sand, which soon raised a very fine cloud This reduced visibility to the extent it was difficult to see the landing area, and we had to exercise extreme caution to make sure you weren't landing on top of another aircraft. After two days of lifting the marines and all their kit ashore, we started to have engine problems.

This started by engines "surging "on start up. Surging is caused by an imbalance of fuel and airflow in the engine resulting in damagingly high jet pipe temperatures and complete loss of power. The surging then started to occur on engaging, and then on reducing power on landing. It was obviously only a question of time until one happened in flight. My last flight was fully laden back to the ship, and a very gentle running landing back on board. It transpired the sand was highly corrosive, and the turbine blades were being eroded to a point where they were no longer efficient. All flying was stopped, but unfortunately several aircraft were stuck ashore!

Fortunately, the RAF aircraft was not affected, and we had one serviceable engine on board the ship which it could carry as an underslung load. Thus, began a series ferry trips and engine changes to bring back the aircraft stuck ashore. An engine change normally took two days, but the maintainers got it down to five hours! Eventually all the aircraft were recovered, but it meant no more flying until the ship got back to UK, and the aircraft could be unloaded by crane. It was an undignified end to a lengthy commision.

Finally having left Aden the ship started the long voyage home non-stop through the Suez Canal. As we had only one serviceable aircraft there was little for the aircrew to do. The plan for the Squadron was for it to be re-equipped with Wessex Mk. 5, and re-embark on Bulwark for a further tour in the Far East. I had assumed I would be part of this, but was surprised and dismayed to be told by the CO that myself and another pilot, Nic Price, would be leaving the Squadron to help form a new one, 826 an anti-submarine unit based on HMS Hermes. Neither of us wished to do this, but we were told we had no choice.

This meant we had to do another conversion course at Culdrose, so after three weeks very welcome leave at home, and another 21st birthday party, I set off for Culdrose in my new car, a second hand Mini.

CHAPTER 6

826 Squadron

I found out later that the Navy at that time was short of experienced helicopter pilots despite the whole course I was joining being destined to join 826 Squadron on its formation. HMS Hermes had been in refit for two years and on commissioning needed four complete new squadrons. Finding the sudden amount of aircrew, both fixed and rotary wing must have been a nightmare for the appointers, hence the decision for the two of us relatively experienced pilots to be transferred. We joined the next Wessex Anti-Submarine course in 706 Squadron at Culdrose at the beginning of November 1965. I had not flown since August in Aden, but rapidly became re-acquainted with the Wessex 1. The airframe was the same as the ones we had been flying on 845, but the autopilot was very different, and the rear cabin was now full of a dipping sonar and two crew, a sonar operator and an Observer, who was in charge of the tactical situation.

The autopilot was designed to bring the aircraft to a 40 ft. hover over the sea, so the sonar transmitter could be lowered. The system then switches to the sonar cable as the datum, to keep it vertical and the right height. This allows the aircraft to operate in all weathers, day or night, normally with two pilots.

The conversion course to anti-submarine flying consisted of two months in 706 Squadron at Culdrose, then two months at 737 Squadron at Portland in Dorset learning tactics, and taking part in the tactical exercises in the exercise areas. It also included a three day detachment to HMS Lofoten in the south west approaches. It was four months of very intensive flying, day and night, getting used to this new environment.

The autopilot was not perfect, and could easily run out of its limited authority. It needed careful monitoring, hence two pilots. The course was also the opportunity to fly with and get to know our new colleagues with whom we were to serve for the next eighteen months.

Having finished at Portland we all went back to Culdrose to commision the new squadron. After commissioning the Squadron needed to work up before embarking on Hermes in the autumn.

The Squadron was equipped with six brand new Wessex 1's, and started an intensive work up of anti-submarine exercises from Culdrose. We also had another two week detachment to HMS Lofoten, off the north coast of Ireland. The detachment was four aircraft, with a long transit via Brawdy, Valley and Ballykelly. Lofoten only had one landing spot, so operating more than one aircraft at a time required some smart management of deck movements, and rapid folding and spreading. On one occasion I was the last aircraft back to find an aircraft jammed on the landing spot. With my fuel getting low, and too far from land to divert, I was wondering where to ditch when they managed to clear it. The landing had to be perfect as I didn't have time to go round again, and a very relieved Senior Pilot, Ken Harding, congratulated me, a most unusual event!

We had no sooner got back from that detachment when we were sent on another one, this time to HMS Victorious which was a large fixed wing carrier. It was built and operated in World War 2 so it was showing its age by this time (1966). We were there to participate in a number of anti-submarine exercises, working with the resident Wessex squadron. It was our first experience of operating with a busy fixed wing programme, and having to fit in. It was also our first experience of carrying out Planeguard duties. This is the rescue helicopter which hovers alongside the Flight Deck during any fixed wing operations, in case of any accidents. We were to become much more familiar when we embarked on our own ship later in the year.

The accommodation on Victorious, as we were visitors, was very basic, so were very keen to disembark to Culdrose, and the ship was equally keen to get rid of us! Inevitably the weather at Culdrose was very poor. The usual "Clamp" of very low cloud/fog was right at the limits, but it was decided we should go. Thanks to an expert Air Traffic controller the stream of 826 aircraft made it safely home. It was good for us to take the aircraft (and us) right down to our limits, and that was one of the occasions when all our training paid off.

I was back at Culdrose for two weeks when I was sent on another detachment, this time to our own ship Hermes, which was carrying out its first fixed wing trials in the Portland areas. A complete helicopter Squadron embarked during this period would only have got in the way, but one for all the passenger transits to and from the shore was useful. I was sent for ten days with one aircraft, an aircrewman and a maintenance crew. It was quite a responsibility for a junior sub-lieutenant to be sent off like this and I felt very pleased to be so trusted. It was a very busy period with many flights between Brawdy, Yeovilton, Portland and the ship, with passengers, some VIP's, mail and stores. There was one night Casevac from the ship to Culdrose at 2am which meant getting me and all the team out of bed to quickly get the aircraft ready. The Captain, T T Lewin later to rise to great heights, called me up to the bridge to thank me, which was typical of him.

The aircraft stayed remarkably serviceable throughout, except for one occasion which caused great alarm on the ship. The Wessex had flotation gear fitted to each main wheel, which consisted of a large rubber globe which automatically inflated on contact with sea water. The aircraft was on deck having its blades quickly spread before the next fixed wing operations, when the flotation gear suddenly operated. Being newly out of refit there was much concern that the ships powerful radar might be responsible when the petty officer responsible for the spreading sheepishly admitted he had dropped a large pin, which freakishly had hit the one small unprotected part of the mechanism and activated it!. The next problem was how to move it, as the hard bags were jammed on the deck. They proved impossible to burst, so eventually the crane lifted it sufficiently to remove them. I then flew the aircraft back to Culdrose for the flotation gear to be replaced by a float marker, and then back to the ship.

After this busy period, back at Culdrose I found the Squadron preparing for the next big event, the whole Hermes Air group participating in the SBAC Farnborough Air Show. It had been decided that while the ship was alongside during August and September the Air group should take up a half hour slot, demonstrating the various capabilities of the Buccaneers, Sea Vixens, Gannets and

Wessex. The fixed wing would work from Yeovilton, and the Wessex from Farnborough itself. The show opened with a mass flypast, which given the speed differential, took some organising and practice. We did our own practice formation at Culdrose. I had been chosen to fly the lead aircraft with the Squadron CO, Lt. Cdr.Duxbury in the left hand seat, so I was responsible for the timing of our arrival, just before a mass arrival of 3 Gannets followed by the two jet formations. Our route after taking off from Farnborough was to fly at low level down the main railway line before turning in for our display. We were low enough to see the train drivers face coming the other way!

We officers were living in the Army mess for visitors, an old fashioned Victorian building, sharing with a Cavalry regiment also passing through, while our sailors were living upstairs in the stables, with the horses downstairs. These arrangements lead to much comment!

The display worked perfectly every day and was the subject of much favourable comment. I little realised that in some 20 years later I would be a member of the Flying Control Committee, and be heavily involved with the flying display.

Returning to Culdrose we carried out an intensive period of anti-submarine flying prior to the whole squadron embarking on Hermes, ready for the big Autumn NATO exercise in the North sea. After just two weeks however I was flown back to Lossiemouth prior to the start of a marathon train journey to Culdrose. I had been selected to carry out a two week course there to become the Squadron Instrument Rating Examiner. I would be responsible for the standard of instrument flying, and also for taking the annual Instrument rating test each pilot has to take. As I have already mentioned I have always enjoyed instrument flying so an intensive two week course learning how to instruct was very enjoyable, and I returned to the squadron newly qualified. While I was away the ship had its first foreign visit to Hamburg, where a great time had been had by all!

After a week back on board the ship spent a week in Rosyth on a maintenance period, so the Squadron disembarked to Arbroath. This was the Fleet Air arm apprentice training school, with its own airfield, so they really welcomed a front line squadron. It also enabled us to carry out some mountain flying practice in the adjacent Scottish Highlands, which was unusual for an anti-submarine squadron. It was also enabled me to undertake a number of Instrument tests, the first ones I had taken. Sometime during this period I was promoted to Lieutenant, which meant a welcome increase in salary. After a period back on board, all the Squadrons disembarked for Christmas leave.

This was the beginning of a very sad period for me, as my younger brother Jim, now at University, was killed in a car crash on Christmas Eve. This had a devastating effect on my parents, and I felt very guilty at having to leave shortly after on a 10 month deployment to the Far East. I was given a few days extra leave, but left with the Squadron in the middle of January 1967.

Soon after arriving in the Gibraltar area the ship was hit by a double tragedy when a Vixen crashed after launch, and the ship then ran in to the rescue helicopter hovering over the scene. Both the pilots were killed, the helicopter one being a particular friend of mine, and I was flying the aircraft that picked up his body. It was difficult for me not to be affected, but there was no option. I was flying again next day. Another Vixen was lost a few days later. It was a terrible start to the deployment.

The ship then operated in the Mediterranean, working with other Nato ships, finishing in Malta for the Easter break. My elder brother was getting married on Easter Saturday and had asked me to be best man. I had to apply for special permission to return to UK, but given the circumstances it was granted. I made it home in time, much to my parents delight, and then made it back to Malta, where the squadron had disembarked to Hal Far. It was my first time in Malta, which I came to know very well later on. At that time there was still a very strong British presence there, with two active airfields and a number of ships based there.

Over the Christmas period it had been decided to withdraw the two Whirlwinds which had made up the ship's flight, and give their Planeguard duties to 826, who were given two extra Wessex. We were now spending a lot more time on Planeguard duties, which it must be admitted was a lot more interesting and exciting than hovering over the sea looking for submarines!

The ship paid an official visit to Athens, so we had a chance to walk round the Parthenon (in the rain). Shortly after we left the Military carried out their coup, and expelled the royal family.

We then moved to the eastern Mediterranean, and worked off Cyprus for two weeks before transiting the Suez Canal at the beginning of May 1967. Arriving off Aden shortly after, the intention being to provide a show of force, along with Victorious, who was on her way home. The situation in Aden was very precarious, as Britain was trying to withdraw and leave a friendly government in charge, while various rebel groups were doing their best to disrupt this.

The fixed wing aircraft were flying armed sorties in support for the Army units who were established in bases in the Radfan Mountains, fighting the rebels. We were tasked with helping the Army with troop lifts, flying to high altitude and dusty strips, but always returning to the ship at night. This was a far cry from the usual flying of an Anti-Submarine squadron, but made a welcome change. We were working with units of the Irish guards, who had no intention of dropping their standards, just because they were in the middle of a shooting war in a remote part of the Radfan. They kindly invited us for lunch in the mess tent, and there on the table was a selection of the Regimental silver!

The flying at hot and high altitude was new to most pilots on the squadron, but I was familiar with it from my Borneo experience. We spent a fortnight on this task, and were reminded why we transited at high altitude when we found a bullet hole in one of the aircraft! The local tribe's men were expert shots with their old fashioned long rifles, as a young Army pilot had found when his little Sioux helicopter was sprayed with bullets, any one of which could have been fatal. He thought it was a great joke, but it was a very near miss.

The ship was eventually released to continue its passage to Singapore, but had got half way at Gan when it was ordered to return to Aden, as the situation there had rapidly deteriorated. A fast trip back with no flying, then back on station at Aden, and a resumption of our military tasks up country.

The ship was finally released again and resumed its fast passage to Singapore, where the squadron disembarked to Sembawang on 22nd June, after nearly two months at sea. During the three week stay in Singapore the whole ship's company had some leave, and Sembawang was an ideal place to relax, with its own swimming pool, and the Officer's Club not far away at the main naval base. I had bought an old car so we had some transport. It had been decided that the pilots would undergo a jungle flying course with the Royal Malaysian Air Force at their base at Sempang, near Kuala Lumpur, with the officers staying in hotels. Of course, being an ex "Jungly" pilot I thought I didn't need any more training. Inevitably I was the only to clip the trees much to the delight of the other pilots.

We were staying in a very old fashioned colonial hotel, with no air conditioning, but high airy rooms and overhead fans They were also serving sponge puddings still in a temperature of 30 degrees c! The British defence attaché had organised a welcome reception for us, where I met a very pretty English girl who lived in Kuala Lumpur with her parents. I was very stricken, and after we moved back down to Singapore I flew back up to KL for the weekend. We communicated for a few weeks, but the affair dwindled away, as these things do in the Navy.

On the less pleasant side we aircrew had to undergo a jungle survival course from Sembawang which involved sleeping overnight in homemade shelters and hammocks. Hacking through primary jungle was extremely fatiguing in the high humidity and temperature, and we were all very relieved when we arrived at the pick up point. I had been very alarmed to find on waking my underpants were covered in blood. During the night a leech had found its way in, and I never felt a thing!

Leaving Singapore after a three week stay there followed an intensive period of flying operations at sea, en route to Hong Kong, via the huge American base in the Philippines at Subic Bay. The war in Vietnam was just getting worse, so it was a very busy place, as was the adjacent airfield. We arrived at Hong Kong for a week's stay. This was before it was a tourist destination, so it was a great place for shopping and eating. Our visit was enlivened by an unexpected request from the Hong Kong police to carry out an assault on a skyscraper in the middle of the city at dawn! This was the Headquarters of the local Communist party, who in recent months had been stirring up much trouble and riots. Landing police on the roof meant they could get to the offices much more quickly than fighting their way up from the ground floor, so the documentary evidence could not be destroyed. We practiced troop drills with the police the day before, and a very tough looking bunch they were. The assault went perfectly, with three aircraft landing the police very rapidly on the limited space. A lot of evidence was found including a large stock of Chairman Mao's little red book, of which we all got a copy.

On a more pleasant side I met a charming BOAC hostess at a small party given by one of their pilots who was ex Fleet Air Arm. This time we did correspond, and I did meet her again on the return to UK. The relationship lasted a few months, but the continuous separation ended it.

Leaving Hong Kong the ship made a fast passage to Fremantle, where once again the welcome and hospitality were tremendous. However en route one of our aircraft ditched. It suffered an engine failure in the hover, so all the crew escaped unharmed, but it started to raise a doubt in our minds, as there was no obvious cause.

It had been decided that the ship should make a non-stop passage from Australia to UK for a maintenance period before a return to the Aden area. As the Suez Canal was closed this meant a long transit round South Africa, with little flying en route. Unfortunately another of our aircraft ditched following a sudden engine failure, but this time the aircraft floated and was recovered, with the hope a cause could be found.

The Squadron disembarked to Culdrose but I remained on board as I was waiting to start my next conversion course, to a Wasp.

CHAPTER 7

❈

829 Squadron

When I was discussing my next appointment with the CO I requested I go to a Wasp flight. This was a small single engine aircraft whose primary role was weapon dropping on a submarine, directed by an outside source, normally the frigate on which it was based. The Ship's Flight was entirely self contained, consisting of six maintainers and a pilot. 829 was the headquarters squadron based at Portland, but the conversion course was with 706 Squadron, back at Culdrose, so after three weeks leave at home I was back there. I had been appointed to HMS Arethusa, a Leander class frigate, destined for a deployment in the West Indies, which suited me perfectly.

My two course mates were Bill Wood and Ben Caesar, both very big men well over 6 foot tall. I felt like a midget beside them!. The conversion course was two months long, about 50 hours. The Wasp was a nice aircraft to fly, very agile as it had to be for the deck landings, but not a great reliability record.

I had used some of that money I had saved on Hermes to buy a second hand sports car, a Triumph Spitfire, which I had always wanted. It proved a little unreliable, but after some proper servicing was much better. On one long journey home the clutch failed around Exeter, but I managed to keep going to the outskirts of Birmingham!

Part of the Flight Commander's course was visits to various Naval Stores depots around the UK, one of which was in Perth. This meant a long car trip north, which we shared, before we finally arrived back at Portland, to join 829 Squadron. The operational part of the course was mainly taking part in Anti- submarine exercises in the Portland areas, and also a lot of deck landings, by day and night. Many of these landings were on HMS Undaunted, an elderly frigate, which had been converted to have a small landing deck aft. There was no hangar, so the ship's main task was training; pilots, Flight Deck officers, and radar controllers. I was to become very familiar with it over the next few months!

I hadn't been long on 829 when I was told my appointment had been changed. No longer was I going to Arethusa in the West Indies, but to HMS Yarmouth. Yarmouth was a Type 12 frigate, which was undergoing a major conversion to carry a Wasp. This conversion in Portsmouth was already running late, but I was to form the Flight at Portland, and be ready to help 829 with numerous short detachments. Needless to say I was very disappointed, but had to make the best of it.

The first detachment was to take part in the Biggin Hill Air display. I had been allocated my own Wasp, XS 533, a standard Mk1, and flew a short display with another naval Wessex. Two weeks later we were despatched to Lee-on-Solent for a week to act as a target for a new tracking system being trialled in the Portsmouth areas, a very intensive period of flying, over six hours in one day.

Then followed a most unusual detachment to the American Air Force base at Bentwaters in Suffolk. This was in support of HMS Undaunted, which was day running from HMS Ganges, the Junior seaman training school near Harwich. We were there to demonstrate Wasp operations, but we also were made use of for a Casevac, and to take the Captain on a visit ashore. On the way back to Portland we stopped at Lee for yet another Air Day demonstration.

Then followed a period of various tasks, mainly training Flight Deck Officers. There was one very pleasant visit to the French naval base at Lanveoc in Brittany, with a very memorable sea food meal.

After such a busy period I was quite ready for two weeks Summer leave, but immediately on return to Portland I was off again to Southend, this time to demonstrate from there at Chatham Navy days.

Although Yarmouth was supposed to be the first of the type 12 conversions, it had been so delayed at Portsmouth (hence my lengthy spell at Portland) that it had been overtaken by HMS Rothesay. She came down to the Portland areas for its First of Class flying trials. It was a chance for me to find out what my own ships characteristics would be like. There were no handling problems, and the facilities for the Flight were excellent, with a large hangar and its own office.

I was then sent on the best detachment so far, two weeks in the West Indies! The ship' main anti-submarine weapon system was the Wasp, carrying homing torpedoes. It was controlled by the ships radar, getting the information from the ship's sonar. Obviously it was crucially important that all these systems, and the operators, were accurate to achieve a drop in the right position. The only place where this was possible to check this was the giant Autec range in the Bahamas. This was on a very deep part of the ocean with sensors all round, and a very accurate radar system. This meant that all parts of the attack could be seen, the aircraft drop, the torpedo splash point and the position of the target submarine. The aim was to do as many runs as possible in the two weeks as the range was very expensive to run. The ship chosen was HMS Sirius, a nearly new Leander class frigate, but like all the other Wasp frigates there was only one pilot. The flying was too intensive for just one pilot so I was lent to the ship as a second pilot. The flying was intensive, I flew over 20 hours in five days both day and night, dropping dozens of practice depth charges.

I joined the ship in Bermuda, flying out from UK on BOAC, and had two days on that lovely island before the ship arrived. The middle weekend of the trial was spent in Fort Lauderdale, where we were invited to a party on the Saturday night. Sirius' Flight commander and myself had a battle for the attentions of one of the girls there. I won and he never forgave me!

I flew back from Nassau and got back to Portland to find that I and my flight were being lined up for an immediate detachment to HMS Hecla, a Survey ship currently working off Northern Ireland. This meant a long transit with several fuel stops, to embark on the ship alongside in Londonderry. This was to take part in an extremely secret trial involving the then brand new Nuclear submarine. The trial had obviously been organised at the last minute and involved fitting a special piece of equipment in the aircraft with its own operator, who had never flown before, and flying around trying to find the submarine in the areas north west of Ireland. Unfortunately the weather did not co-operate, the first day was in a Gale force 8, and the next day force 9. The Survey ships were not good sea boats, and the deck motion made flying impossible. On the last day of the trial we made two flights, but whether the equipment worked or not I never found out.

I was particularly frustrated to be sent on this trial as I had a long standing promise to act as best man for a friend of mine from 845 and 826 who was getting married in Liverpool on the Saturday following the trial. It looked impossible, but I found there was a flight from Belfast to Liverpool late on Saturday morning, and I managed to get a car from Ballykelly in time to catch it. By changing in a taxi en route I managed to get to the church half way through the service, but in time to make my speech at the reception. I had no idea how I was going to get back to Ballykelly by Monday morning to fly the aircraft back to Portland. Extremely luckily one of the wedding guests was driving south that night, and offered to drop me off at my parent's house in Birmingham. The next day I could catch a flight from Birmingham back to Belfast, and then by car to Ballykelly, then on the Monday the long flight back to Portland.

During my time at Portland my aircraft was also available for the Squadron flying programme, and on November 15th it was taken by another pilot, Simon Lawrie, on a routine training flight over Lyme Bay. It was a filthy November day, low cloud, drizzle and strong winds. The aircraft suddenly disappeared from radar, and no trace of it was found on the surface, despite an intense search. Some weeks later the wreckage was recovered from the sea bed, and it was found that a bearing had failed at the rear of the engine, and the free power turbine had departed, cutting the tail rotor control cables at the same time. So poor Simon had been faced with a simultaneous engine and tail rotor failure, a quite impossible situation. Later on we found the weakness of that bearing was known about, and a modification had been introduced, but had not been incorporated on that engine.

I had been extremely fortunate, as I had done most of the previous six months flying on that aircraft, including a night flight two days before, and yet the fates had decreed that I was not onboard on that fateful day. It was the closest shave of my career.

Life had to go on and I was sent on another intensive trial, this time based in Guernsey. It was a trial fit of MAD equipment to the Wasp (Magnetic Anomaly Detector). This was another piece of equipment to detect submarines by detecting the magnetic field around it. It consisted of a bomb shaped device being towed behind and below the aircraft. We were working from Guernsey as there are large areas of natural magnetic anomalies in the Channel in that area. The equipment worked correctly, but was never fitted to the Wasp, but it was to the Lynx and Sea King, with moderate success.

Yarmouth's refit was finally complete, and she arrived in the Portland areas, ready for the inspections, and then the six week work up. The Flight had been given a new replacement aircraft, XV 624. This was fitted with the latest equipment including the new AS12 missile system. This was the Navy's reply to the small craft fitted with missiles, especially the Russian Komar class. It was wire guided, aimed by an operator through a sight, fitted in the left seat. The sight was also a simulator, so the operator could keep in practice. We were the first flight to be so fitted, so it gave the ship another weapon system.

The work up at Portland in January and February was really hard and unpleasant, but we passed, and became an operational part of the Fleet. We took delivery of our new aircraft and started to get involved in anti FPB exercises as well as anti-submarine ones. We had a week's visit to Gibraltar where the ship was carrying out wind flow trials, and I carried out a reconnaissance of possible landing sites on the top of the Rock which meant some interesting flying away from the perpetual exercises!

The ship also paid its first visit to its Named town, Yarmouth in Suffolk, where it was made very welcome. The sea was too shallow for the ship to come alongside, so it anchored off the pier, and used the ship's boats. They weren't suitable for the Mayoral visit, so I was tasked to land in a park and pick her up. As she was a middle aged lady the biggest problem was getting her in to the aircraft, so I had a special set of steps made, which worked fine. I had never been to that part of England before. Little did I know that in four years time I was to return there to get married!

While I had been based for so long at Portland I had become very friendly with a girl from Weymouth, and she was not impressed with my imminent departure for ten months! However we promised to write, which we did faithfully, and wait to see what happened on my return.

After another period of training at Portland, the ship finally left for its Far East deployment on June 10th 1969. After the Arab- Israeli wars the Suez Canal was still closed, so we had a long solo transit round South Africa, refuelling at Madeira, Freetown in Liberia, off Ascension Island and Cape Town. This meant lengthy periods at sea, and only the chance to exercise our selves, but we had plenty to do to keep in practice for all our roles.

We stopped for three days at the Naval base at Simonstown, which is about 12 miles from Cape Town. This was at the height of Apartheid in South Africa, so it was not a very pleasant place to be. I flew ashore to the Air base at Ysterplaat which was the base for the South African Air Force Wasps, one of the few other countries to buy that aircraft.

After our short stay we set off again to take up our next task, the Beira Patrol.

When Rhodesia (now Zimbabwe) declared independence various sanctions were applied, including all fuel oils. This was circumvented by oil being brought in through Mozambique, through the port of Beira. Directed by the UN, Britain established a blockade by RN ships to prevent any imports. The Patrol had started with an aircraft carrier but by 1969 it had been cut down to two frigates and a giant oil tanker to provide fuel. After one unsuccessful attempt there had been no other attempts, so there was very little for the ships to do. The biggest problem was boredom, as each ship had a four to six week spell.

We carried on with our usual exercises, and I did quite a lot of flying transferring mail with the other frigate and the tanker, but the month on station did drag. The boredom was relieved by a week's visit to Mombasa, where the Naafi had a rest camp called Silversands on a delightful beach some miles north of the city. It really was a tropical paradise to sleep in huts, to the sound of waves breaking on the coral reef a perfect place to relax away from the ship for a few days. That area of beaches is now full of luxury hotels where I later spent a family holiday but at that time it was completely unspoiled. I organised a one day safari for the Flight to the Tsavo National park which went down very well.

On the way to Mombasa we passed the Comoro Islands, a little known French possession in the Indian Ocean. I flew the Captain ashore for his official visit, and then I had the chance to fly round the island to discover a very active volcano in the middle. It was quite a thrill to look down into the crater to see pools of molten lava, and lots of smoke. It was not a place to have an engine failure!

Soon we were back on the Beira Patrol for another month, nothing had changed, it was just as boring as the first time. We were finally relieved to make the crossing to Singapore, stopping at Gan to refuel. We arrived in Singapore three months after leaving UK, and yet again I disembarked to Sembawang.

Once again Sembawang was the ideal place for a rest after such a long period at sea. There was the Far East spare Wasp there, which we could fly while mine was being maintained, carrying out the work which was more difficult to do on board, and all the crew could relax a little before we set off again on the long passage to Australia to take part in a large exercise in the Pacific, starting in Sydney. There was much exercising en route, particularly with our two "chummy" frigates, Galatea and Rothesay, with which we had also shared the Beira Patrol. The ship was due to spend some time in Sydney before the Exercise so I disembarked to the Naval Air station at Nowra, about 100 miles south of Sydney. While I was there I flew a long navigation trip inland to Canberra. I also had the opportunity to fly in an Australian UH1-B helicopter which at that time was in action in Viet-Nam.

I also had the chance to visit my friends whose wedding in Liverpool I very nearly missed, now teaching in a town just north of Sydney, which was a very pleasant break.

I re embarked again prior to the big exercise, which we were not looking forward to, as it was going to long periods at alert, ready to fly, and the weather forecast was awful. Fortunately the ship suffered a major boiler problem, and was forced to stay in Sydney, so we missed the exercise!

The ship was due to spend Christmas in Hong Kong, and en route exercised with the other RN ships which had been taking part in the exercise we missed. One flight was to ferry Flag Officer Second in Command Far East fleet back to his ship. It turned out to be Admiral Lewin, my previous Captain on Hermes. I also had the chance to fly over the Great Barrier Reef, but the number of sharks I could see in the clear water discouraged me from hanging around!

The ship spent two weeks in Hong Kong over Christmas so I disembarked the flight to the small RAF base at Kai Tak, the huge international airport. I had several flights along the border with China, being very careful not to cross it! I was also asked to fly Father Christmas (one of the ship's Chiefs) in to the middle of the HK cricket ground for a huge charity children's party. This needed special permission from the HK CAA, who issued me with a unique document authorising it.

Leaving Hong Kong the ship sailed straight back to Singapore, exercising en route, particularly in our new role of missile carrier. This included some live SS11 firings and another stay at Sembawang. On re-embarking we started to have engine problems, which necessitated an engine change with the spare engine we carried on board. That also turned out to have a fault, so we arranged to take Galatea's spare. Unfortunately during the ensuing engine run the Flight Petty officer, "Tex" Ritter, an outstanding technician, got too close to the engine intake and the airflow ripped off the pocket off his jacket, which went down the intake. Another engine change! This time we had to use the Far East spare engine, kept at Sembawang. This was flown out to us by underslung load by a Wessex of 847 Squadron, now based there. We had been very fortunate on the trip so far, with very little unserviceability so this episode challenged the Flight. Three engine changes in two days!

Finally leaving Singapore we set off back across the Indian Ocean for another spell on the Beira Patrol. In our absence little had changed. Our month spell there really seemed to drag, despite a lot of flying. Finally being relieved we set off home back round the Cape, stopping at Simonstown again. On the long trip north the ship refuelled from Tankers strategically placed. They must have had a very tedious time stuck in the middle of the Atlantic. I flew ashore to Freetown to collect the mail, but after that we had an undercarriage problem which could ot be solved until we received a spare oleo in Gibraltar. The ship finally got back to UK on 14th April, having been away 10 months.

During all this time my girl friend and I had been writing, and so we were very pleased to see each other again. I was sharing a small cottage with my friend Roger Bryant, prior to my ship's departure again for the Mediterranean. We were to take part in the big annual Nato exercise, Dawn Patrol, with my old ship HMS Hermes .Our spell in the Mediterranean was improved by a visit from my girlfriend to Malta for a few days. She surprised me by turning up at the ship's official cocktail party on the island of Gozo. I also had a few days at home from Gibraltar to attend the interviews for entry to the Empire Test Pilot's school, but more of that later.

It was a very busy time, broken by a spell as guardship to the Royal Yacht at Cowes week. As I couldn't fly during this period I was given the job as Foreign ships liaison officer which kept me very busy. We also had another visit to Great Yarmouth, and another flight for the Mayor out to the ship. We then set off for another Nato exercise, Northern Wedding, This time with Ark Royal, complete with her new squadron of Phantoms. The exercise was held in the north of Norway, and the weather was very poor, with very rough seas, but with a visit to Oslo at the end. We then returned to Portland where I was expecting to stay for a few weeks until we went out to the Med again for another Nato exercise. However I did not know that one of my colleagues on HMS Rothesay had been ill, and they urgently needed a replacement as they were working as the safety ship for the brand new nuclear submarine, HMS Churchill. Once again this was in the Atlantic, off Northern Ireland. After another long trip north I joined the ship in Glasgow for a very busy fortnight in the Atlantic working with the submarine. I had to go and fetch the mail twice from Ballykelly in the middle of the night, as the ship had to close the land from the exercise areas. On one of those flights I nearly had a collision with an RAF Shackleton aircraft which mistook my orange anti-collision light for a marker buoy they were looking for! Every time I turned away they followed me. They then had the temerity to put in an Airmiss report, blaming me!

I was glad to get back to Portland for a few days before embarking again on Yarmouth bound for the Mediterranean again.

Once again we were working with Ark Royal, and also with other frigates, especially Galatea and Rothesay which we had with us in the Far East, and the Atlantic. The exercise, "Lime Jug", was in the eastern Mediterranean around Crete, and Yarmouth was frequently acting as Planeguard for the night flying on Ark Royal. As usual the Ark was being shadowed by a Russian frigate, which normally stayed a safe distance away, but on the night of November 9th badly miscalculated and crossed in front of the carrier, which was working up to speed for a launch. They collided, fortunately a glancing blow which pushed the Russian out of the way, without cutting it in half, or rolling it over.

Several of the crew were knocked in to the water, which in November was very cold. Several boats were launched, one very chaotically by the Russian. Some of the men were picked up, but some refused to get in to the British boats at first, such was the power of their conditioning, despite their dire predicament. We spent the next two days searching but found nothing. It was very nearly a major disaster and international incident.

The ship then proceeded to Malta for the exercise debrief, as it was only for a short time the flight did not disembark, so the ship was alongside when we had an emergency call to take a doctor to a British tanker, Esso Chile, which had had an explosion on board, and a badly burnt casualty. We were the only helicopter on the island, and fortunately the ship was not too far away. I flew to the naval hospital to pick up the naval doctor, and winched him down to the ship, which unfortunately did not have a landing spot. While we waited the doctor decided it was imperative the casualty was taken to hospital as quickly as possible. This posed a problem. On a proper SAR aircraft the winchman would be lowered to the ship, to be winched back up with the casualty, the winch being controlled by another crewman. There was only my crewman with me so we worked out a scheme where I controlled the winch and lowered the crewman to the ship, where he connected up the stretcher, and I winched him back up on a series of hand signals from the ship. This worked very well and the crewman was able to just get the stretcher in the aircraft, and we took him to the hospital. By this time we were very low on fuel, so I rushed back to the ship.

We never did find out if the casualty survived, but Esso were so grateful they sent a cheque for £50 to the Flight, who were all in favour of a big party, but I decided a pewter mug each would be a better souvenir!

The ship then returned to the Uk, with a visit to Rotterdam en route. My friend and Flight Deck Officer, Jim Macrae, also the Supply Officer, had some friends in Bonn. They invited us to a party there on the Saturday night, and when we found out there was a direct train from Rotterdam we decided to go. We had a great time, but their current boy friends were a bit put out! We made it back to the ship the next day.

My time on Yarmouth Flight was coming to an end after two years, and I had asked for my next appointment to be as a Staff pilot on 829 Squadron at Portland. This would give me a chance to apply again for The Empire Test Pilot School at Boscombe Down (ETPS), as my first attempt had failed, and it also gave me a year ashore. Just prior to me leaving Yarmouth paid a visit to Newcastle, where the whole cast of Hair was entertained in the Wardroom, and drank the bar dry, much to the annoyance of the Captain. The next day I took off from the ship alongside to return to Portland, straight into low cloud. After a while of flying in solid cloud I realised we had to divert somewhere and fortunately made contact with the RAF airfields in Yorkshire, and was given a radar approach to Church Fenton. I was very pleased to get down. The next day we made it back to Portland with two more refuelling stops.

So began my time ashore as a Staff Pilot. Much of my flying was training and testing others, particularly instrument flying and deck landings. I had one trip away to Birmingham on a recruiting drive at their annual show, which also gave me a chance to see my parents. Landing a helicopter in the middle of a public park next door to the dog show caused a good deal of upset, as the resulting down draught ruined their carefully arranged hair styles!

I was also sent on a Helicopter Weapons Instructors course, which I thought was a good thing to do, in case my application to ETPS failed. The course consisted a period of six weeks theory at the Naval Gunnery school at Whale Island in Portsmouth, followed by four weeks at Culdrose flying with 707 Squadron. I got caught up in a game of politics between 829 and 707 Squadrons. HWI's had to be qualified as AS 12 missile aimers. As I have mentioned Yarmouth was the first Flight to be issued with this wire guided missile which was guided by an operator through a sight. It was quite a skilled job, and the operator kept in practice by using a simulator which worked through the sight, exactly as if he was firing a missile. The aptitude test for this was driving a spot of light around a chart on the wall. After much practice I was passed as suitable by the HWI on 829 at Portland. After the six weeks at Portsmouth I was assessed again at Culdrose by the 707 HWI prior to a live firing and was deemed not suitable! I was then returned to 829 as a staff pilot having somewhat wasted eight weeks.

I applied again for the ETPS course, and was called again for the intensive interviews at Boscombe Down. This time I was much more prepared and had done a lot of reading up, so was delighted when after a few weeks I was told I had been selected. This meant a four year period ashore, one year on the course, and three years on the Helicopter test squadron. Privately this suited me perfectly as I was still seeing the same girl friend from Weymouth, and we had had a very happy holiday together in Corfu in the summer time. So once again I packed up my Ford Cortina and set off for a new experience of test flying, which was to play such an important part in my life.

CHAPTER 8

Empire Test Pilot's School

The Empire Test Pilot's School was formed in 1944 to train experienced pilots to be able to assess and comment on an aircraft's flight characteristics and its suitability, or otherwise, for it's proposed role. The first course was purely for British and Empire pilots, but that soon changed and the second course had two Chinese officers as well as other foreigners. This mixture has continued ever since, with roughly half the course now taken up by pilots of friendly nations. On my course in 1972 we had pilots from the USA, Australia, France, Israel, South Africa, and Germany, as well as those from all three British services. It was a great benefit of the course to get to know and fly with pilots from very different backgrounds. As I have mentioned selection for the course required an above average flying ability, and the need to pass the very testing interviews.

Being unmarried I lived in the very comfortable Officers Mess, with a lady servant to look after me. I had two rooms, one bedroom and a study/lounge in which to work. I soon needed this as the Ground school work started straight away with three weeks of solid Mathematics and Aerodynamics, which was a sharp reminder what was ahead in the coming year. Fortunately having passed A-level Maths I could just about manage, but some of the others struggled, particularly the foreign students. The course was difficult enough for us in English, even more so if it was a foreign language. The Chief Ground Instructor, Squadron Leader John Rogers, was excellent, giving help and guidance where necessary, but a rapid pace was expected. This initial Ground school lasted three weeks, with an exam at the end. After this period the routine was a ground school lesson at 0830, and then the flying for the rest of the day.

I was part of No. 10 Helicopter course, and there were six of us; two RAF Flight Lieutenants, Stuart Collins and Paul Buckland, an Army Captain, Mike Barrat, Rod Dean from the South African Air Force, and Gunter Sprenger a German civilian. As the year progressed we all became firm friends. A lot of the flying was mutual, so we mostly flew with two pilots, one doing the flying, and one recording, as well as running the instrumentation. The course was divided into separate sections, each one requiring a hand written report, within ten days of finishing the flying on that exercise. The School had three aircraft, a Scout a Whirlwind Mk. 10, and a Wessex 1. I familiar with the Wessex of course, and the Scout was a land based variant of the Wasp. The Whirlwind was a turbine powered version of the Mk 7 I was familiar with. While we were doing our familiariarisation flying on these, we started our first exercise.

The first exercise was a non-flying one, the Cockpit assessment. This was a detailed examination of a cockpit layout, showing how it could be improved. In my case I was given the Scout with a very old fashioned cockpit layout, designed in the 1950's, and not dissimilar to the Wasp, with which of course I was very familiar. This was my first introduction to report writing. They all had to be in the approved format and hand written, which inevitably meant working all evening. Living in the Mess I soon settled into the routine; cup of tea and toast at 4.30, two hours work, then Dinner at 7.30. Back to work at 8 for a couple of hours, then a short spell in the bar with the other students. This worked well for me but how the married students managed to fit in the work with their domestic duties I have no idea.

The first report written and very proudly handed in to be marked, it was quite a shock to have it criticised and covered in red ink. We had two helicopter tutors, Lt. Cdr Mike Hope and Squadron Leader Trevor Egginton. Little did I realise that I was to continue my association and friendship with Trevor for the next 40 years. He was a major figure and inspiration in my career. The tutors were there to guide and assist us as well as flying with us on the initial flight for each exercise, demonstrating the techniques required, and both of them were excellent in doing this.

The exercises frequently overlapped, and one could be finishing the flying on one exercise while still writing the report on the last one. The first flying exercise we did was one of the basic test requirements establishing the errors in the pitot/static system. This was achieved by towing a "bomb" below the aircraft in clean air. It was also our introduction to having to fly extremely accurately, holding speed and altitude to very tight limits for a three minute period. While we were flying this on the Whirlwind we also started on the Flight envelope assessment on the same aircraft. Flight envelope is the speed and altitude limits that the aircraft is permitted to achieve at various weights and centres of gravity, so there was quite a lot of flying to do. As well as all this we started the climb performance on the Scout, which involved climbing up to 16000 feet, well above the normal limit of 10000 feet. This involved using oxygen for the first time and finding the Scout had a minimum speed of 48 knots and a maximum speed of 54 knots at 16000 feet. It felt like the aircraft was balancing on a pinhead, and I felt I was only marginally in control! Fortunately we did this flight with one of the tutors, but the climbs at slightly lower altitudes we flew with a fellow student.

One of the many benefits of the Course was the chance to fly, and pilot, the many different types of aircraft in the School fleet. After just three weeks there I got the chance to fly in the Argosy, a large four engine freighter. I was the co-pilot of course but had the chance to do a lot of the handling, including a number of circuits at St. Mawgan, culminating in a simulated double engine failure! I also flew in the Hunter trainer, a fast jet fighter, which was a great thrill.

The next exercise was an assessment of take offs and landings. This sounds simple, but involved some 5 hours flying, and a very long report. At the same time we were measuring the level flight performance in the Scout, so it was a very busy time.

Another unusual task we had to complete was to fly three hours in the School gliders. There were two, one a two seat trainer, in which we had a very short check out, and a single seat high performance German one. These were towed airborne by the school Chipmunk, also flown by us. It was nine years since I had flown a Chipmunk, but after a short check out off we were sent towing a glider for the very first time, towing a fellow student also on very nearly his first time! We had to do the gliding at the weekends in our own time, so we were very keen to stay airborne as long as possible to get our three hours in. In Gliding you are totally dependent on the weather, and I was very fortunate on my third flight to be towed over to Compton Abbas, a small grass airfield to the west of Boscombe. It was the perfect day for gliding, even for a novice like myself. There were so many thermals, I had trouble getting down at the end of my hour. The flight concluded with my first glider land away at Compton. I was very lucky to complete my three hours in one weekend, as well as doing a lot of towing. It was a unique experience, typical of ETPS.

It was now June, and we were halfway through the course. There was no let up in the pressure, and the next exercise was Engine Off Landings. Through my entire career so far I had flown single engine helicopters, so practising for an engine failure was a frequent part of training. All helicopters can auto rotate, which is the equivalent of gliding in a fixed wing aircraft, so there is a gentle controlled descent, and a slow speed touchdown. Only instructors were allowed to carry out an actual engine off landing, so all the times I had done one I was never quite sure whether the instructor had intervened a fraction of a second before me. At ETPS we flew the exercise with another student, so there was no doubt that you were doing all the flying! Closing the throttle on my first attempt was one of the bravest things I ever did. Our assessment was flying at various speeds, and flaring at different heights. We also assessed how long we could leave the controls before intervening, simulating a pilot caught by surprise. This was quite a dangerous exercise, as if you left it too long the rotor may have slowed down the point where it may not recover! Fortunately we flew the exercise in the Whirlwind, which was very forgiving, and we all completed the exercise with no damage to the aircraft.

I also had the chance to fly in another of the ETPS fleet, this time the supersonic Lightning. This was a great thrill and fulfilled a long standing ambition to fly beyond Mach 1. The aircraft was the two seater training version and of course we flew with one of the tutors. The take off was dramatic with a rapid climb to 50000 feet. The acceleration to supersonic was down the Channel, and although I was flying it I felt as if I was some miles behind the aircraft! The landing speed was very fast, and landing was quite beyond my ability. All in all it was very memorable, but I was glad I had chosen helicopters.

I was also co-pilot for another long range flight in the Argosy. This only cruised at 180 knots, so the flight from Gibraltar to Gutersloh in Germany took six hours. The next day, a Sunday, we cruised around Germany for three hours, returning to Boscombe the next day. These long airways flights cured me of any lingering desire to be an airline pilot.

The next test exercise was measuring the longitudinal stability of the Wessex. This involved a series of aft pitch inputs, and measuring the resulting aircraft reaction. This is a measure of the aircraft's manoeuvrability, to an international standard. One had to be very cautious, as too much of an input could chop the tail off! At the same time as flying and reporting on this very complicated exercise, we were still finishing the autorotation and engine off exercise, and starting the engine assessment on the Scout. It was a very pressurised time.

Another unusual test was measuring the hover performance of the Whirlwind. This is called tethered hovering, and involves cables of different lengths being secured to the load lifting hook of the helicopter, the other end secured to a load measuring gauge secured to the ground. The aircraft then lifts in to the hover until the cable is vertical and increases the power in stages while the load is measured. This will give the power required for different hover heights and aircraft weights. This was a whole course activity, as it had to take place on a windless day, and as well as the two pilots in the aircraft two guides are needed to ensure the cable is vertical and another to measure the loads on the cable. Each condition had to be held steady for two minutes which was very difficult as the aircraft liked to bounce on the cable until a steady condition was achieved.

Vitally important of course was the need to disconnect the cable before moving away, as there was no weak link in the system. Some years after our time when a Sea King was carrying out the exercise this was forgotten. The aircraft tried to move away, pivoted on the cable and crashed. The aircraft was written off. These exercises took us to the long summer break, which was sorely needed.

I had become very friendly with one of the few other bachelors on the course who also lived in the Mess, Terry Farquarson of the Australian Air Force. As he could not go home I invited him to spend a few days at my parent's house, so he could see a bit more of England. We had a day trip to Stratford, and were lucky enough to get tickets for the Theatre there, where we saw a performance of Julius Caesar. Terry and I maintained our friend ship long after ETPS and still keep in contact today.

On returning to Boscombe for the final term of the course I was very upset to find one of the course members, Mike Barratt of the Army Air Corp, had left. It must have been very hard for him after all the hard work of the first two terms. He and I, being strangers at a large RAF base, had felt a close affinity, and I had been looking forward to working together for the next three years.

One of the many features of the Course was the visits to industry, to learn what new developments were coming along, and to make contact with the industry test pilots with whom we would be working in the future. We were normally very well entertained on these visits, as the firms knew that we might be in position in future to comment on their products. We visited all the major firms, Rolls-Royce, British Aerospace where Concord was being assembled, and of course Westland Helicopters. We also visited several of the smaller firms who were sub-contractors like Plesseys and Louis-Newmarks, who made helicopter autopilots. We normally travelled by coach, but if it was a long distance we travelled in one of the Schools fleet.

We were now starting the third term with only two more exercises before starting the culmination of the Course, the Preview. This is when we are given ten hours flying on a type of aircraft we had not flown before, and comment on its suitability for its role, using all the knowledge we had gained on the course.

The last two exercises were assessing the lateral and directional stability of the Wessex, and the Instrument Flying capability of the Scout. The instrument flying I found particularly interesting with my background as an instructor and examiner, flying with my fellow students, and seeing how they managed. The Scout had no autopilot to assist you, and a very poor instrument layout, so there was much to comment on. As well as these two exercises we also carried out a mini preview on the Seaking, a large two engine naval helicopter. We only had two hours to carry out a detailed handling assessment of this large and complicated aircraft. After just three hours flying we were judged competent to captain the aircraft! We then had only ten days to submit a very detailed report. It was excellent practice for the proper Preview we were about to embark on. It was not something we could have contemplated a few months previously.

For the Preview we were split in to Syndicates; in my case I was working with Paul Buckland and Gunter Sprenger, and we were previewing the Puma, a medium sized helicopter in service with the Royal Air Force as a tactical troop carrier. We carried this out at RAF Odiham with 230 Squadron, and we had a week to carry out the flying, then ten days to submit a very lengthy report covering every aspect of the aircraft, and also prepare a presentation.

All our flying was with the Squadron CO, who was obviously determined, we didn't break his aircraft! We split the task between us, each one taking some of tests we had learnt about on the course. I took the handling qualities, some of which meant going up to 10000 feet, and putting in control inputs to see the reaction of the aircraft, not something the average squadron pilot would do. I also carried out the autopilot and instrument flying assessment, and helped Paul with the tactical flying. Gunter did the engine and performance tests, at which he excelled, his graphs were masterpieces.

After five days of intense activity we returned to Boscombe and started writing. As the report had to be typed we had to allow extra time to take the drafts to the typing pool, where the girls there were magnificent, as the report was well over 200 pages, and we were on a very tight time schedule. However we made it within the time limit, and then were able to concentrate on the presentation. This had to be exactly 30 minutes long, and present our results to an audience consisting of the rest of the course, some specialists from Boscombe, and of course visitors from 230 Squadron.

We were very proud of our achievement, and were delighted when we won the Hawker Hunter trophy for the best presentation. This was presented to us at the formal dinner, marking the end of the course, and we all went our separate ways. I, and the other two RAF officers on the course were destined to join the Rotary wing test Squadron at Boscombe.

During the Summer of the course I had become engaged to my long term girl friend. We had managed to stay together through all my absences, but we couldn't agree when it came to buying a house. We eventually split up just as I was occupied in the Preview, which was less than ideal. Perhaps we had been together too long without moving forward. She eventually married another Naval helicopter pilot who unfortunately was killed in the Falklands.

CHAPTER 9

D Squadron Boscombe Down

During my three years on the rotary wing test squadron at Boscombe, I was fortunate enough to be there when two new types of helicopter were coming through, the Lynx and the Gazelle. I was also involved in two lengthy icing trials in Canada and a number of deck landing trials.

Initially I was quickly converted onto two new types, the Gazelle and the Wessex 2. I then carried out a number of radio trials on these aircraft, which were not very challenging from the pilot's point of view, but enable me to become familiar with the aircraft. I was going to fly the Gazelle for a number of years in various forms, it was always a favourite of mine. It was a delight to handle but only some versions had an autopilot, so it was hands on the controls at all times.

Following the radio trials, I was then sent on my first visit to Ottawa in Canada where the squadron was carrying out icing trials on three different types, the Sea King, Scout and Wessex 5. At the same time the Gazelle was carrying out cold weather trials, investigating a handling problem which had occurred on the aircraft's introduction into service with the Army.

The main aim of the icing trails was to establish if it was possible to give the aircraft a clearance to fly in icing conditions, which occur frequently in Northern Europe. It had been a task for Boscombe for several years and the trial I was sent on was one of several previous attempts. The trials were based at Ottawa as there was an experimental spray rig there which sprayed fine droplets over the helicopter which was hovering adjacent to it. In temperatures below zero it was similar to flying in icing cloud but at a safe height if there were problems. It was ideal for the initial exposures but at some point it was necessary to expose the aircraft to the real thing.

There were several aspects to icing in helicopters. Firstly, the engines must be protected from ice ingress. On some engines a small piece of ice can damage the turbine to such an extent that it is not producing power at all, so it was vital to prevent any ice ingress at all. Most engines have some sort of ice protection system built in, normally a hot air bleed to the first stages of the turbine to prevent ice from forming on the turbine itself.

Further ice forms on the leading edge of rotor blades, as it would on a wing. This affects the airflow, increasing the drag and increasing the power required. The trials were trying to establish if a limited amount of ice could be permitted and how that could be indicated to the pilot. At the same time the engine protection and other systems could be assessed.

My particular project was the Scout which I had already flown at ETPS. Just flying the Scout in cloud was quite a challenge as it had no autopilot but watching the ice accrue added a new dimension. The Scout had a small highly loaded rotor so any ice had a noticeable effect, particularly in autorotation so this had to be checked every few minutes.

To achieve it the engine had to be split off by closing the throttle, all this while rapidly descending in cloud! Perhaps it was not surprising that I was given this task as the new boy. Normally this very complicated task would be flown by two pilots but in this case the left hand seat was occupied by a scientific trials officer.

The trials showed that the ice had such an effect on the rotor blades that it was impossible to give a clearance to the Scout to fly in icing conditions, although the engine was well protected. It was a rather negative result but showed that not all trials were successful. The other aircraft on trial, the Sea King and Wessex 5, were concentrating on engine protection. The equipment on trial for them was successful on the Wessex but not for the Sea King, which meant it would have to go back to Canada next year to try a different method.

The other aircraft I flew a lot was the Gazelle, newly into Service. It was carrying out Cold trials rather than icing, particularly with the effect on the control system. This was a simply hydraulic system to assist the pilot by nullifying the forces on the controls. It was possible to fly the aircraft with the hydraulics switched off but the control forces were very high. It had been found that these forces increased with a reduction in temperature, to the point where the pilot could no longer overcome them. Our trial was to see if there was a temperature below which the aircraft should not be flying. This meant a lot of flying with the hydraulic system switched off, simulating failure. We always flew these sorties with two pilots, as on several occasions the control forces were greater than I could overcome. It was all great experience for a test pilot beginner.

As there was no Service accommodation for us in Ottawa we lived in furnished apartments in the city centre.

These were very comfortable and a big improvement on normal service quarters. It did mean we had to cook for ourselves but we all managed surprisingly well! The trial finished with the advent of warmer weather and we were all ferried back to Boscombe in the Britannia which was kept there just to support foreign trials. It was the last one in Service use. The rather slow overnight trip was marked by my first view of the Northern Lights.

I had hardly been back two weeks when I was asked to go to Marignan, the airfield near Marseille, to take part in some engine trials on the Gazelle. Marignan is the home of the Aerospatiale factory. Aerospatiale had the design authority for the Gazelle, so this was a joint trial, with French test pilots. The aim was to check the engine acceleration characteristics at high levels. As I was going out for the trial and there was a requirement to ferry out a Gazelle to Marignan I was asked to take it, helped by a Naval Observer who was also based at Boscombe. There appeared to be a great urgency for this so we set off on a Friday, stopped at Orleans for lunch and overnighted in Vichy. The next morning, Saturday, we flew the last leg to Marignan, arriving at lunchtime to find the whole factory shut. We were met by a solitary Frenchman who put the aircraft straight into a hangar and couldn't get rid of us fast enough! I had a few days to wait before the arrival of the rest of the Boscombe team, so I set off to explore Marseille, which I had never visited before. This included a delicious lobster lunch at a restaurant down by the harbour. That night I suffered terrible food poisoning and spent the next two days in bed at the hotel, barely recovering in time to start the trial.

The trial was engine accelerations at altitude, starting at 10000 feet which was the maximum in the UK. The regulations in UK also insist that oxygen is used for any flying above 10000 feet. This is cheerfully ignored in France and the trial was cleared up to 13500 feet. A French test pilot accompanied me on all the flights to demonstrate the modification we were assessing, so that was a great help.

On returning to Boscombe I found I was being lined up for my first deck trial, which was with the Gazelle on board the Naval ship RFA Engadine. Engadine was the ship used for deck landing practice, it had taken over the role of HMS Lofoten which I have mentioned previously but was built specially for the role. Most unusually this was a manufacturer's trial (in this case Aerospatiale) in which we were participating. The manufacturer is not normally involved in operational trials like these, but this was a first for the Gazelle so very sensibly a completely joint trial was set up. The Aerospatiale test pilot Bernard Pasquet, with whom I got on very well and the initial trials were held in the Portland areas. Unfortunately to progress further, we needed stronger winds and the winds in the Channel were very light, so it was decided to move further north, off the Hebrides. Once we got there, we found the light winds had followed us, so it was decided to try again later in the year.

Back to the Gazelle, we were still investigating the stick forces and also a new requirement, hydraulic jack stall. This occurs when during a violent manoeuvre the forces back from the rotor overcome the power of the hydraulic jacks and the controls suddenly stiffen. It had already been the cause of an accident to an Army aircraft but was very difficult to repeat, as it varied from aircraft to aircraft and with the violence of the manoeuvre. Our task was to try and establish a limit to impose on the aircraft to prevent it occurring.

I was also back flying a Wasp again, carrying out carriage and dropping trials of the new Mk 44 torpedo. These had to be carried out on a range at Culdrose in Cornwall and the aircraft returned to Boscombe. I was getting rather nervous as the return date was getting rather close to my Wedding Day in East Anglia!

Following the end of my previous relationship, through mutual friends, I had met Margaret and not long after got engaged. Her parents, an ex-Naval officer, lived in Beccles in Suffolk and the wedding was in a small country church nearby. It was a military wedding with my colleagues from the Squadron forming a multi-Service guard of honour. The weather was perfect and we were able to squeeze in a four day honeymoon in Torquay before moving in to our new home near Blandford in Dorset. Margaret was a nurse and was able to find a job at a practice in Blandford, while I commuted the 30 miles to Boscombe. I was very happy in my job there and found the flying interesting and challenging.

My next task, as well as settling down to married life, was more radio trials in the Gazelle and the completion of the deck trials on Engadine, this time with much stronger winds. I also had my first flight in a Lynx, a type which I was to fly for the next 35 years, in various forms. This was in the first protype XW835, with my friend and colleague Stewart Collins, who had been on the ETPS course with me and had also been best man at my wedding. I was not very impressed, it was underpowered and had uncomfortable levels of vibration but these were normal features of a first prototype.

Then followed a busy period of Gazelle trials, including the first encounter with the Stability Augmentation System, which was a lower level of autopilot. It was fitted to the RAF and Naval versions to help in obtaining a clearance to fly in cloud. Towards the end of the year I started to fly the icing trials Sea King, which I was going to fly to Canada on the next trials after Christmas.

As well as the modern aircraft I was flying, there was a Whirlwind 7 at Boscombe, which we used for continuation and instrument flying. I had not flown one since Borneo seven years previously but it soon came back to me especially as I was the Squadron instrument rating examiner and used it frequently. It was the last Mk 7 in Service and was looked after by a small party of sailors, who eventually I was responsible for. I never had any problems with them, as they thought they had the best job in the Navy!

The next icing trials in Ottawa involved a Sea King, Wessex 5 and Puma. I was responsible for the Sea King and the main task was to assess the ice deflector fitted above the cockpit, nicknamed "The Barn Door". This was a simple Sikorsky modification which had been in service for some years, especially with the Norwegians who regularly flew in icing conditions. I had been sent to Norway a few weeks previously to fly with them and seen their confidence in it. Our trial was a little late starting as the RAF Belfast aircraft (the only type large enough to carry a Sea King) was delayed crossing the Atlantic and we were not able to start trials flying until the beginning of February. Once we did start we did a lot of snow flying and flying in natural icing. It soon transpired that the Barn door did its job of preventing ice entering the engine intake but in mixed conditions ice and slush formed on the front of it and some sort of ice protection was necessary on the Barn Door itself. A liquid de-icing fluid system was incorporated and the subsequent trials next year proved the system and the Sea King was eventually granted an icing and snow clearance.

On the domestic side we were living in apartments again but this time much more modern and comfortable. We were lucky enough for my new bride to obtain a flight to Ottawa and she came and joined me, a great adventure for her. One of the great features of Ottawa was the Rideau Canal which went through the entire city and of course in winter was frozen solid. The surface was cleared and thus provided a seven mile skating rink, so we all bought skates and learned how to use them. I was never very comfortable with them and often ended up in the snow banks on the edge of the canal.

The Canadians take fire very seriously, particularly when the temperature outside is -20C. So, when the building fire alarm went off at 11pm at first we ignored it, until someone was pounding on the door, telling us to get out. Our flat was on the tenth floor so it took some time going down the emergency stairs with everyone else in their night clothes! We found a very embarrassed member of our team being very forcibly debriefed by a very large Canadian fireman who took a dim view of fire alarms being set off by accident.

I had been called back early to participate in the first Lynx deck trials, which were being held on a French ship, the Tourville. Once again, this was a joint manufacturer's trail, in which we had been invited to participate. The French were partners in the Lynx programme, so they had provided the ship which was working out of the French port Lorient. There was no accommodation on the ship, so we were staying at a hotel in Lorient and being ferried out to the ship, which meant early starts and late finishes. I had flown a very short conversion flight on the prototype with the then Westlands Chief Test Pilot, Ron Gellatly and then a familiarisation flight on the Naval version, XX 510, with the Westlands project pilot, John Morton. They then very trustingly allowed me to go off by myself, so I became the first Royal Naval pilot to fly the Lynx.

The trial showed that even at this early stage the Lynx's deck landing capability was excellent and this was proved many times in the years to come.

This was my first occasion of working with Westlands, who were to play such a major part in my later life.

On my return I was involved in a very different trial, assessing a modification to the Sea King engines to give it more power in hot climates. My co-pilot for this was an Australian naval pilot, Keith Engelsman, who had been a fellow student on my basic flying training course on Chipmunks. He had completed the ETPS course the year after me and had been sent to D Squadron while he was waiting to accept some more Australian Sea Kings, which would also have the modified engines. Our paths had crossed several times over the years, at various locations around the world, so I was very pleased to fly with him again.

During my time at Boscombe I was contemplating my own career. I had joined the Navy on a Short Service commission, which meant retiring at aged 37, with the option to leave after 5, 8, or 10 years. I hadn't wanted to leave after 5 or 8 years and the 10 year point came up as I was starting ETPS, so I was committed to staying in until I was 37, with a very small chance of staying in longer. However, if I was to transfer to a full service commission, I could stay in until 55, with a much greater chance of promotion. Having just got married and thinking of the future, I decided to apply to transfer, even though I was a long way out of the normal zone. I was strongly encouraged by the squadron CO, Commander "Buster" Bale and was very pleased to be transferred to the General List in 1974.

The meant that eventually I would have to go back to sea in a non-flying job and learn all about ship handling and navigation, so I could eventually become Captain of a ship, which is the ultimate ambition of all General Service seaman officers. Meanwhile I would carry on at Boscombe concentrating especially on the Lynx, to aid its entry into service.

Then began an intensive period of Lynx flying in two of the early prototypes, the first Naval version and the first Army version, XX 153. Many of these flights were with a Naval Observer, Tim Howard-Jones, who was to become a firm friend. He was assessing the radar on the aircraft, which was used as the new control radar for the Sea Skua anti-ship missile.

These were interrupted by an intensive deck trial on board the RFA Olmeda, a large tanker which had just had a major alteration to the structure immediately forward of the flight deck, which had altered the airflow over the flight deck.

There had been reports of the pilots having difficulty and our job was to see if a new release was required. We used a Wessex 3 borrowed from the Navy, with personnel from a ship's flight to support it. The trial was in the South West approaches in December, so conditions were just right, with strong winds. Olmeda proved to be a very difficult ship to work from as it was very long and the Flight Deck was very high, so the ship's motion was accentuated. We soon found that the new superstructure had a marked effect on the wind over the deck, so it was not surprising the Service pilots were having difficulty. It is the job of the test pilot to establish where the limits are and then establish a margin for the Service. It is very difficult to work up to a limit without occasionally going over it, especially in a very dynamic situation like a Deck Landing and I managed to do that when landing in one of the worst wind conditions. I had to use more power than the permitted maximum to control the landing. Fortunately it was only for a few seconds as was shown on the instrumentation we had specially fitted for the trial, so no damage was done but the ships flight took a very dim view of what I had done to their aircraft! The trial was a success, with over 170 landings in the nine day period and we had enough data to issue a new safer release.

Although in the winter of 1974/5 there was another icing and snow trial I could not participate in as I was involved in another deck trial, this time in a Wasp on the then new Type 22 frigate, HMS Amazon. This was much more straight forward and we managed over 100 landings in a three day period, resulting in a very satisfactory release.

Then followed a relatively quiet period which was just as well as my wife was expecting our first born and I was preparing for two more deck trials, both on the new Type 22 frigate, HMS Sheffield. One was for a Wasp release and the other was for the Lynx, the first deck landings on a British ship. The Wasp trial was in June so there was the usual problem of light winds. We were seeking them in the North Sea, when a small fishing boat was sighted on fire. I was sent off to investigate, accompanied by a fellow Boscombe test pilot, David Beswick, who as to become a lifelong friend. The fishing boat was not occupied and I had just given my opinion to the ship that it should float for a lot longer when it sank! David has never forgotten the incident. The Wasp trial was cut short to prepare for the much more important Lynx trial.

There was much interest in the trial as of course the Lynx had been designed as the Wasp replacement, with particular emphasis on the deck landing ability. To help achieve this it had a strong three leg undercarriage, the ability to apply negative thrust to hold the aircraft on deck and most important of all a harpoon which was engaged in a grid on the deck after landing. The Wasp had a deck release to hold it on deck before take off but nothing on landing. It was obviously important to land on the correct position, or the harpoon could not engage, so I had carefully briefed the Flight Deck Officer, under whose direction I was landing. Unfortunately, we didn't get it quite right and missed the grid on the very first landing but the Flight Deck Officer soon became familiar with the positioning and all the following landings were successful. These landings confirmed my first impressions and the Lynx went on to become a very successful small ship helicopter, with customers worldwide. HMS Sheffield had the misfortune to be sunk in the Falklands campaign seven years later.

As I have mentioned there was a small detachment of Royal Navy personnel at Boscombe with a Commander as the Senior Naval Officer, who was usually also the Commanding Officer of the Rotary Wing Test Squadron. When I joined in 1972 there was also a Naval Staff Officer to help in the naval administration. This position was a hangover from the days when there was a naval test squadron at Boscombe, with a large number of naval personnel. This position was filled by a retired officer of great character, Terry Lovell, who was not overworked but who was quite happy! About two years into my time there, Terry suddenly died and I found myself doing his job as well as mine, as there was no intention to replace him. It was good experience for me to get back to Naval matters before I left Boscombe. About this time I was promoted to Lieutenant Commander, which meant a welcome pay increase.

I then flew an intensive period flying from Portland in the second naval Lynx prototype, XX910, which was the trials aircraft for the Seaspray radar. This radar was to provide targeting information for the Sea Skua missiles which would eventually be fitted to the Lynx but was also useful in other roles. Most of the radar trials were in the Portland sea areas with Tim Howard-Jones but I was also looking at other aspects of the Lynx, including handling and engine work. A new navigation system was also fitted to the Lynx, the Decca Tactical Navigation System or TANS. After years of flying the Wasp with no navigation assistance this was a revelation, at last the pilot had his own and his ship's position available to him.

This was my last trial at Boscombe, I had three very happy years there and had flown 12 different types of helicopter. No other job could have offered me that type of experience but it was time to move onto my next appointment which was very different. I left with a glowing accolade from the Superintendent of Flying and the eventual award of the Queen's Commendation for Valuable Services in the Air.

CHAPTER 10

HMS London

As I mentioned before I had transferred to the General List and now had to undergo a period of sea training. I had been informed that with all my unique experience on the Lynx my next flying appointment would be as a Senior Pilot of the first Lynx squadron, in September 1976. I was appointed to HMS London as assistant Navigation Officer for a period of seven months. The main objective was to obtain my Bridge Watch keeping and Ocean Navigation Certificates which were the basic requirements for any future command.

London was a large destroyer of County Class, whose main armament was the Sea Slug missile and two 4.5 gun turrets. It was much larger that the frigates I had served in, about 4500 tons and was powered by two steam boilers and a brand new idea, four gas turbines.

I was working under and being trained by, the Navigating Officer, David Irvine who was to prove a stern by fair teacher. I had had no experience at all of ship handling or ocean navigation, so I had a lot to learn. The Captain, Peter Nichol made me very welcome and I settled down to life back on board. The Royal Navy is a great equaliser; at Boscombe I had been responsible for the latest multi-million helicopter project and on London I was given responsibility for the gang way furniture. I was left in no doubt which was the more important!

The ship had just finished three years in dockyard hands and was starting to come to life again. Shortly after I joined we started a series of trials working out of Portsmouth and then a passage to Gibraltar for further ships trials. My place of work was on the bridge. Either all the time when Special Sea Duty Men were required (when entering or leaving harbour), or as a second Officer of the Watch when on passage. The passage to Gibraltar was the first one I planned and I found it was not too different from the many long distance flights I had carried out. It was very important to arrive at the destination at the exactly the right time and work back from that to work out the correct course and speed. I was continually checking that, as well as watch keeping. As we were close to the coast on this trip, there was no need for the celestial navigation we would need for the ocean passages but I started to become familiar with a sextant.

I was also working in other parts of the ship, one of which was the foc'sle, at the bow of the ship. The officer in charge was Frank Allica, an Australian on exchange. One windy morning sailing from Gibraltar the cable to tug pulling us off the jetty suddenly parted and snaked across the deck, fortunately without hitting anyone. It was a salutary lesson on how quickly a dangerous situation can arise at sea. Frank became a great friend and our paths were to cross many years later.

Returning to the UK the ship was preparing for its work up period at Portland. This is a six week spell of intensive

Hiller 12 E

Whirlwind Mk 7 – 705 Squadron

PP5 with H.M.S. Norfolk

PP5 with Westland built Spitfire

First flight PP5 with PP3

Airspur Westland 30 California

The first 2 production Westland 30

Merlin deck trials H.M.S. Iron Duke

PP4 the ill fated avionics test aircraft

Whirlwind Mk 10 ETPS

First Flight of PP1 October 1987

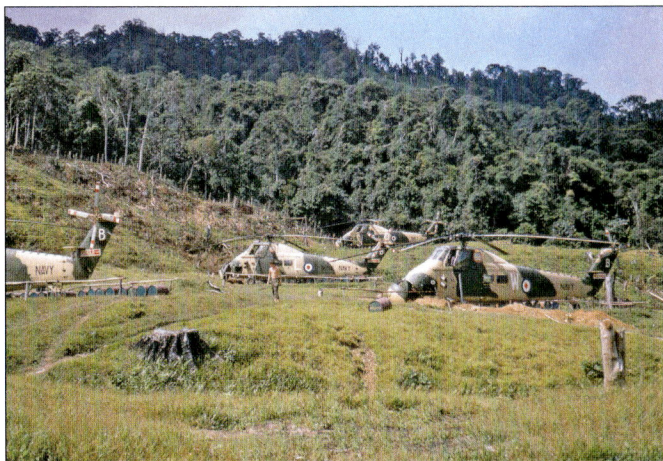

Wessex 1 of 845 squadron at Nanga Gaat Borneo

Typical landing site Borneo

Visit of HRH Duke of Edinburgh

Last helicopter flight with my two sons

training in every aspect of the ship's operations, which it must pass before it can join the fleet. It is a very tiring period, with early starts and late finishes and I spent nearly all the time on the bridge.

The ship's flight was embarked with a Wessex 3 which I had flown at Boscombe but I was careful not to get involved, although I did manage two short flights in my time on board, just to prove I hadn't forgotten how to do it!

Having completed Workup at Portland and passed, the ship was now preparing for its major event, a visit to New York to take part in a huge Naval review to celebrate the Bicentenary, the two hundredth anniversary of the signing of the Declaration of Independence. The review consisted of a rendezvous with over fifty ships from twenty one different nations 180 miles off New York and forming a column 20 miles long to enter New York. We were anchored in the Hudson River about halfway up the line, ready for a review from the President the next day. The passages across the Atlantic had been given to me to plan as an exercise in celestial navigation using the age old methods of sextant and star charts. This meant taking star sights at dawn and dusk every day and ensuring the ship was on time for the rendezvous. I was quite familiar with the procedure by now and found great satisfaction in correctly using the data to plot the ship's position. It was even more important than usual to get the timings and our position right with so many other ships involved. Just to add to the pressure we had the First Sea Lord embarked, Admiral Ashmore. We joined the long line of ships waiting to enter New York harbour, until we reached our anchorage position on the Hudson River. I was on the radar to give the exact position to the Navigating Officer who was finally responsible and between us we got it right.

I had little time to enjoy New York, as I was busy planning the return trip. We were going straight to the firing range at Aberporth in West Wales for the ships annual Sea Slug firing. This was a major event as the Sea Slug was the ship's primary weapon system, indeed the ship was built around it. As part of my training I had been acting as deputy to the officer in charge of the firing, so I was looking forward to seeing the system work, as we had many practice firings before the live one. On the afternoon of the firing with half an hour to go the officer in charge, who had been enormously stressed, declared himself unfit and went back to his cabin. The Captain asked me if I was happy to carry on, which I was, so we carried on, fortunately with a successful result.

Half way through our time at Aberporth the ship had to anchor in Fishguard harbour for an overnight stay and I was given the task of planning the approach to this as part of my qualification. Having prepared it I then had to con the ship myself, being carefully watched by the Captain and the Navigating Officer. It all went well and we finished up in the right position, although the approach had been a bit fast, more like a helicopter manoeuvre than a ship's!

On completion of the firing the ship was returning to Portsmouth for Summer leave. I was due to leave the ship for my next appointment and was very pleased to be awarded my Watch keeping and Ocean Navigation Certificates by the Captain, so all the hard work had been worth it but I was very pleased to be going back to flying.

CHAPTER 11

700L Squadron

When the Royal Navy accepts a new type of aircraft the first squadron is called an Intensive Flying Trials Unit, or IFTU and its main task is to fly as many hours as possible to prove there is no latent defect the Manufacturer may not have discovered. It is also intended to train the first aircrew and ground crew and start to evolve new tactics and operational procedures. In our case, the aircraft was the Lynx Mk 2, which was the Wasp replacement on small ships. As well as carrying homing torpedoes like the Wasp it was also due to be fitted with a new anti-ship missile, the Sea Skua which was guided by the Lynx's radar, although this programme was running very late.

The Lynx IFTU was given the name 700L Squadron and was manned by specially selected Pilots and Observers. It was unique in that it was jointly manned by personnel from the Royal Dutch Navy, as they had also ordered the Lynx to replace their Wasp fleet. The Squadron were allocated the first production aircraft as they came off the production line at Westlands in Yeovil and very conveniently were based at Yeovilton, seven miles up the road.

As I have mentioned, I was involved in the early Lynx development at Boscombe so it was to be expected that I was appointed as the Senior Pilot. My responsibilities included training the other pilots and for producing the daily flying programme, which was intensive. The first two aircraft were planned to fly 100 hours a month and the remaining three British and two Dutch aircraft 50 hours a month. As the normal flying rate on a Squadron was about 30 hours a month, it can be seen the task was very challenging. The first aircraft, XZ 229 was received in September 1976 and the Squadron would finish in December 1977, when it would become the first Naval Lynx Squadron and the first Ship's flights would form.

I had the task of accepting each aircraft from Westlands and then starting the pilot conversion. Some of the pilots had completed a conversion at Westland, including the new Commanding Officer, Geof Cavalier. We had known each other since my time on Wasps and had shared a flat together, so we knew each other pretty well. My opposite number, the Senior Observer, Rob Green, was an ex Sea King man, we shared an office together and worked very closely for the whole of the IFTU. In fact there was very little for the Observers to do initially, as the first two aircraft had dual controls and no radar.

The Dutch contingent consisted of a joint Commanding Officer, Puck Venjer and three pilots, Willem Onrust, Jan Pasman and Ivan Krijns. The squadron was completely integrated and all the aircraft were flown by all the pilots. The Dutch primary role was search and rescue, so all their aircraft had dual controls and they always flew with two pilots, with the second pilot cross trained as an Observer.

The second British aircraft, XZ 230 arrived at the end of October 1976 and the first Dutch aircraft, 260 a month later. By now we were well into intensive flying, trying for each aircraft to fly six hours a day, generally in two hour sorties. We had prepared a series of flight profiles, trying to represent the way the aircraft will operate when in service. By now I had converted three pilots on to the Lynx and with the Dutch pilots and some more Observers we were not short of aircrew. I was kept very busy, for as well as planning and supervising the programme, I was flying as much as I could. The third aircraft, XZ 231, I had a problem accepting, as it had a vertical bounce on the ground, which Westlands could not explain. We sent it back to them for rectification and we got it back a month later. We also received the second Dutch aircraft, 261, which was immediately incorporated into the flying programme.

So far with five aircraft we had had very few incidents, so I was not too surprised to suffer our first engine failure. We were over the Bristol Channel when I noticed one of the engine's oil pressure start to fall. The Gem engine will not run for long without oil, so I shut it down and diverted to the nearest airfield, which was Chivenor on the north coast of Devon. Chivenor was not longer an active airfield but an RAF SAR flight was based there. They made us very welcome, while we called for help from the Squadron. The side of the aircraft was covered in oil, so it looked like a major leak. However, on investigation it transpired that when topping up oil prior to our flight, the filler cap had not been replaced correctly, so that was where the oil was coming from, a great relief! I flew the aircraft back to Yeovilton the next day.

There we two more incidents which resulted in emergency landings, the first one was an indication of low oil pressure in the main rotor gearbox. This is a very serious emergency and the advice is to land as soon as possible.

In this case the aircraft was operating in the middle of the Bristol Channel, the pilot decided to land on the island of Flatholm. Although there was a lighthouse station there with a phone, it was the worse place he could have chosen if we had to recover the aircraft. I was sent with orders to get it back to Yeovilton somehow. I was flown out to Flatholm with a technical team to find it was an indication problem. The main gearbox has two separate pressure indications, one to a gauge and the second to a warning light. In this case it was the sensor to the gauge which was faulty, so changing it solved the problem and I was able to fly the aircraft home.

The second incident was more serious but also involved the main gearbox oil system. The aircraft was operating over Lyme Bay when it had genuine indications of loss of oil. This time the pilot landed in a field on the top of the cliff near Seaton in Devon. Yet again I was sent out with a technical team to recover the aircraft. This time the problem was much more serious, a metal pipe had split, so the oil loss and indications were genuine. This meant fitting a new pipe but the only way to get one was from Westlands. As there were no spares of this pipe, one had to be robbed from the build line. This took time, so it would not be available until next morning. By this time it was getting dark and it was obvious I was not going to get back to Yeovilton. The owner of the land, who had been taking a great interest in all this, offered me a bed for the night in the local manor house! He also took me down to the local pub in Axmouth where, still in my flying overalls, I was treated like a visitor from outer space! The next morning, with a new pipe fitted, I flew the aircraft back to Yeovilton.

By this time we had received all the British aircraft and the Dutch contingent returned to Holland, after what had been a unique and successful joint squadron. May 1977 was about the mid point for the IFTU and was marked by a week's detachment of four aircraft to RFA Engadine, for a very intensive period of flying in the South West approaches. This was an opportunity to start developing new tactics for the missile firing, even though we knew this would be long after the conclusion of the IFTU. I also carried out the trial of the internal overload fuel tank, on a flight lasting four hours and twenty minutes, which was the longest in my career. I flew this with my friend Dave Beswick, who had taken my place at Boscombe Down.

The next major event was in June 1977, the twenty fifth anniversary of the Queen's accession to the throne. This was marked by the Royal Navy with a Fleet review at Spithead, with a fly past of all the Fleet Air Arm aircraft, fixed wing and helicopters. The big fixed wing formations where due to fly past first, followed immediately by the helicopters slightly lower. We were due to be second in the formation, after the Gazelles of 705 Squadron from Culdrose and followed by large formations of Wessex and Sea Kings, also from Culdrose. We all landed at Lee-on-Solent, with the intention of taking off from there, flying round the Isle of Wight and flying over Spithead from the east. This was the good weather routine, which we rehearsed and was only slightly modified for bad weather. Come the day and the weather along the south coast was awful, low cloud, mist and drizzle. Our four aircraft made it to Lee, to find the Gazelles already there. The Staff Officer in charge then hurriedly changed the plan so that we were now first, in the belief we were better equipped to find our way round the Isle of Wight to be on time! On setting off we found the cloud base was only about 200 feet but fortunately getting higher as we went further east. We hoped the larger helicopters were joining in behind, the fixed wing were circling above the cloud unable to descend and participate, much to their frustration. We made it on top of the Royal Yacht exactly on time and then separated to get back into Yeovilton under radar control. The Queen was very pleased apparently but it was very nearly a complete disaster.

The next few months were very busy, as the IFTU was drawing to a close and we tried to pack in as much flying as we could. This also included Yeovilton and Portland Air Days and joining in many of the exercises in the Portland areas. The highlight was when we were asked to fly Lord Mountbatten from Greenwich to his home near Romsey. He had been to a Mess Dinner the night before, so wasn't feeling too well. He didn't realise he was on a live intercom, so we had him coughing and spluttering all the way, so we had little chance of conversation. He was very grateful and wrote me a charming thank you letter.

As the IFTU came to a close I had to make some important career choices. During 1977 our second son was born, so with two little boys at home, I wasn't too keen on long separations. As I mentioned I had worked quite closely with Westland Helicopters and had got to know the test pilots office quite well. It was still a surprise when the Chief Test Pilot, Roy Moxam, invited me into his office and offered me a job as a test pilot. I was coming to the end of my time on the IFTU which had gone very well. We had flown thousands of hours and had not lost an aircraft or aircrew. The final push was another ten day detachment to Engadine, during which I had made a mistake and damaged an engine. In retrospect, I was probably very tired and distracted but there was no excuse. The IFTU was well rewarded, the Commanding Officer, Senior Observer and Engineering officer all got promoted and I got my next appointment, the Flight Commander of HMS Kent, a DLG like HMS London. This was very similar to the job I had been doing ten years ago, when I would have been expecting the command of a squadron, so I was a little disappointed. The Westland job meant less time away from home, a more settled life and a change to carry on flying, especially test flying, which I much enjoyed. I accepted the offer.

Now came the difficult bit. Having gone to a lot of trouble to obtain a permanent commission, I now wanted to resign. I didn't want to do that until I had a firm offer from Westlands. This took a little while to arrive and meanwhile I had to start my new job at Portland. Although I had flown the Wessex 3 at Boscombe, I still had to go through the two month conversion at Portland. Normally, if one resigned, you left after a few months, in my case, I was told to wait for a suitable time in the ship's programme, which wasn't until she came back from a South American visit in May 1979, fifteen months after I had put in my letter. Fortunately, Westlands were happy to hold the job open for me and as long as I joined before my 35th birthday on 10th June, which had an effect on my pension, I was content. Obviously, I had to maintain my enthusiasm for the job, or that would rapidly affect the efficiency of the Flight, so I had no option but to carry on.

CHAPTER 12

❊

HMS Kent Flight

A DLG Flight consists of 12 maintainers, lead by a Senior Maintenance rating, normally a very experienced Chief Petty Officer.

Operating a Wessex 3 from a DLG had one particular difficulty, the positioning of the hangar. As I have mentioned the ship is designed around the Sea slug missile system. The launcher is at the stern of the ship but the large aerial which controls the missile has to be as close as possible to the launcher, so is on some superstructure, just in front of the Flight Deck, which also has to be near the stern. The hangar which would normally be directly in front of the flight deck, is thus in front of the aerial superstructure, so the aircraft is stowed by directing it to one side, with a wheel in a guiding channel. Then by the way of two turntables, it is fed into the hangar. This is difficult enough when the ship is stable but with the ship movement and darkness it becomes very difficult indeed. It is not surprising that the aircraft is often secured on deck rather than in the hangar.

The Wessex 3's main role is anti-submarine and it has a very powerful sonar which is lowered into the water. It is normally manned by a crew of four, the first pilot (me), the co-pilot normally a sub-lieutenant on his first tour, an Observer and a sonar operator. I was lucky enough to inherit Mike Burleigh as co-pilot, Eddie Dobinson, a very experienced Observer and Petty Officer "Sharky" Ward, also very experienced as Sonar operator. We operated very well together for the next ten months.

I joined Kent at the beginning of April 1978 when the ship had just come out of a Maintenance period. At the height of the Cold War she was involved in many large Nato exercises, all of which had a large submarine element and inevitable contact with Russian ships. The Captain of Kent was an ex-submarine CO, "Shorty" Turner, who was short in stature but large in personality. He knew nothing about aviation, so was happy to let me get on with it.

Our first task was to shadow a Russian task force on its way home round the north of Norway. The force included included their new Aircraft Carrier, Kiev, so we were keen to get as much intelligence as possible. We had been given a special camera, so the plan was to arrive unannounced, with radio and radar silence for us and the ship. We were operating very like a Swordfish in WW2! Having failed to find Kiev, we got back to where we thought the ship should be, to find no sign of it. We were getting short on fuel and I was contemplating our only diversion was the remote island of St. Kilda, which we held on our radar, which by now we had turned on. That would have been extremely embarrassing, as there was no fuel there. However, shortly after we did find the ship, who had been listening to our calls and eventually replied having given us a scare. We did eventually find Kiev and her escorts and got some good pictures, by which time we were north of the Arctic Circle.

After that the ship put into Rosyth for ten days, during which we disembarked to RAF Turnhouse, which is now Edinburgh Airport but was then a very quiet joint RAF/RN unit which ran the joint JMC exercise we were about to embark on in the North Sea. JMC 782 was a large 10 day exercise involving many ships and aircraft. We were airborne every day and night. When it was finished the ship had a 6 day visit to Hull where we were made very welcome. The sailors particularly enjoyed the dance that was put on for them. The ship then embarked on a cruise in the Baltic, with visits to Copenhagen and Stockholm, both of which was made more enjoyable by perfect May weather. En route we passed close to the Polish coast and came across several Soviet ships obviously involved in an exercise. We lowered our Sonar and soon detected a submarine, the first and only time we knew for certain we had found a Russian one! It must have been puzzled by our presence as it surfaced shortly after and turned out to be a very unusual looking one, a Whisky Longbin class, by now rather obsolete.

During our visit to Stockholm we were honoured by a visit from the King, who seemed a very pleasant and unassuming man. On our return to Portsmouth the ship took part in a series of Sea Days, which was a demonstration of the ships capability to the Press and foreign dignitaries, including a flying display.

The ship then moved to the west coast of Scotland for a series of firing trials, using a small pilotless aircraft as a target. The recovery of this had always meant using a sea boat, for which the ship had to stop. We devised a method of recovery using the aircraft's winch and freight hook, lowering a ship's diver to connect up a long strop to the PTA. We used this method several times very successfully. After a very busy July we returned to Portland for two weeks Summer leave.

The ship was planned for a three month maintenance period in Portsmouth Dockyard but for various reasons this was sub-contracted to a private shipyard on the Tyne. During this four month period we were disembarked at Portland, taking part in the numerous exercises there. We had a change in co-pilot, David Heelas joining us for his first tour.

This period ashore was very useful for me as were involved in selling our house and buying a new one near Sherborne, near to my new job. Unfortunately it wasn't nearly ready before I had to go on a three month deployment to Brazil, so we had to move temporarily into Married Quarters in Weymouth, where my family stayed during my absence.

We re-embarked on Kent at the end of January prior to a very intensive three week mini work up to Portland. The ship had a new Captain, John Gunning, an Observer, whom I had met before. At the end of February we set off on our 10000 mile journey.

First stop was Gibraltar where we joined up with the other ships that were to accompany us. The next visit was to Lagos in Nigeria, the first time an RN ship had visited there in a long time. It turned out to be a very dangerous place to be, not somewhere you could have a quiet trip ashore and three days was quite long enough.

En route to Ascension Island we were going to refuel, we carried out another unannounced reconnaissance visit to another new Russian Aircraft Carrier, Minsk, which was on its way from the Baltic to their Far East fleet. Our paths happened to cross mid-Atlantic and this time it worked. We came across the ship on a Sunday morning with the crew on the Flight Deck relaxing, including the Squadron dog. Our unexpected arrival seemed to cause a lot of upset but we took a number of excellent photographs of this new ship. On our way back to Kent we were told by the ship's radar we had company! After we landed a Russian helicopter arrived alongside, obviously been sent to find out where we had come from. They must have been sent in a hurry as the pilot was only wearing shorts and sandals. We exchanged a cheery wave before he departed. Approaching the Brazilian coast we carried out a number of anti-submarine exercises before arriving at our main destination, Rio de Janeiro.

Rio was everything we were expecting. I was looking forward to it as it was almost my last foreign visit in the RN. However just before we arrived, I was told the officer deputed to be the visit liaison officer had to go home and I now had the job, as obviously I would not be flying during the visit! This meant organising all the trips and social visits and took up most of my time. However, it did mean I worked closely with the Brazilian liaison officer and we become good friends, to the extent I was invited to dinner at this flat with his family. The highlight of the visit was the train up the mountain with the statue of Christ at the summit. The views of the city and the Sugar Loaf Mountain were fabulous.

After a week in Rio we sailed for the main purpose of our visit, joint exercises with the Brazilian Navy, Brasex. These were mainly anti-submarine in which we participated but also naval gunfire support, where we spotted for a Brazilian destroyer of World War 2 vintage. We never did see the fall of shot so could only hope they didn't hit anything! After another short visit to Rio for the debriefs we set off on the long journey home. As I was leaving the Navy on our return I was rather put out to have the Flight inspection by the Admiral's staff. It was very difficult to maintain the correct enthusiasm which was expected, but I managed it and we passed satisfactorily, which I suppose was good note to finish on.

We called at the port of Recife for our final visit. This was marked by a trip to the local circus, which was just the same as the ones we used to have. After that it was full speed for Portland and final disembarkation on May 17th 1979. After returning all my equipment and handing over to my relief, I was free to leave the Royal Navy after nearly 17 years.

CHAPTER 13

Westland Helicopters

I joined Westland Helicopters at the beginning of June 1979, a few days before my 35th birthday. This was important to me as the pension scheme was based on your final salary, with a retirement age of 55, and if you had completed 20 years service, you got the maximum pension of 50% of your final salary, so I was very pleased to have just made it.

I was made very welcome by the other pilots, some of whom were coming to the end of their career, John Morton and Don Farquarson, both very experienced from whom I learnt a lot. Some of the others I knew already, Stuart Collins (my best man), joined just before me as did Derek Marpole, with whom I had served at Boscombe. There were some pilots I hadn't met before, one of them being Jerry Tracy who was to become a particular friend over the years.

My salary on joining was about the same as I had been receiving in the Navy, which enabled me to take out a mortgage on the new house we had just purchased.

The first thing I had to do was obtain my civil licences. In the previous months when I had been at sea I had been working on a correspondence course for the licences set by a firm called Avigation, based in Ealing in the London suburbs, run by Mr. Nabarro, brother of the well known MP. This culminated in a two week intensive refresher course, just before the seven exams I had to take in London. Other students were very much like me, ex-service pilots working to obtain their licences. I became very friendly with an ex-Vulcan pilot, Vic Nightingale, and we kept each other going through the fortnight.

Roy Moxam, the Chief Test Pilot, very generously covered the expenses for the course, the exams and the accommodation. So for my first two months at Westlands, I was working in my new office on my exam preparation, with no flying. One very pleasant surprise was the announcement that the test pilots were joining the Company car scheme, and I was entitled to choose a brand new car! The level of car was based on your ranking in the firm, so I was very content to have a large family saloon.

Having worked so hard on the exams I was very disappointed to fail one, The Rules of the Air. This was one I hadn't done much work on as I thought I knew them, but it was a short exam in which you had to get every question right. However I could take it again in a month's time, and this time I passed, and got my licences. Meanwhile Roy had realised that I didn't need civil licences to fly Ministry aircraft, which was by far the majority at Westlands, so I flew my first aircraft as a civil test pilot on 14th August 1979, a Lynx Mk. 1, XZ 213, on its initial flight. This was a new form of flying for me, carrying out an Air Test Schedule, or ATS, on brand new aircraft to make sure it met the customer's contractual requirements. It was always a great thrill for me to make a first flight, and there were rarely any problems, such was the quality of manufacture at Westlands.

I had always assumed that it would be a while before I was trusted with any development flying, but my second flight was in one of the prototype Lynx on a high all up weight trial. The development engines on this aircraft were very underpowered, so it needed careful management. I was very pleased to be trusted with this, and did all the flying to complete the trial, as well as continuing the ATS (Air Test Schedule) on Lynx Mk 2, and Dutch aircraft.

I also participated in the trial of a very early helmet sight, where the pilot is looking through his visor which has flight information projected on it, the idea being he does not have to glance down in to the cockpit. I was never comfortable with this concept, and found myself either looking at the sight, or outside, but not together. It was not helpful that the sight was mounted on a temporary frame which was excruciatingly uncomfortable. Since then of course the principle has been refined and this system of helmet mounted display is a standard fit on modern fighters.

Sea Kings were still in production and it was not long until I was flying them again, having not flown one since Boscombe four years previously. It was a pleasure to get back into the large machine, my first one being a Mk. 3 for the Royal Air Force. Westlands had sold a large number of Sea Kings to India, the Mk. 42 in the Anti-submarine role, and they had come back to order an up rated version, the 42A with different weapon systems. It had been decided that this version should operate from Frigates, and would thus need a haul down system to assist the pilot in landing.

The haul down system was developed by a Canadian firm for their S.61's to routinely operate from their frigates. As well as assisting the landings the system, called Beartrap, also moved the aircraft into the hangar. The Indian system did not have this facility, only the haul down, and

Westlands had the responsibility for the design and fitting to the aircraft. I was very pleased to be made the project pilot for this, as I had a lot of deck landing experience with Wasp, Lynx and Wessex aircraft. A complete test facility had been built at the western end of the airfield, so I started a series of trials flights.

The system works by the pilot lowering a messenger cable from the aircraft, which is connected on the ground to the haul down cable. This is then hauled back in to the aircraft and locked in to the housing mounted on the under surface. This housing was positioned directly under the centre of the main rotor head, so the aircraft would be guided down in a level attitude. There was a series of warning lights, so the pilot knows when the haul down cable is locked in. Gentle tension is then applied to the haul down cable until the aircraft is centred over the deck, and then more tension is applied to gently pull the aircraft down to the deck. Once on the deck high tension is applied to hold the aircraft on deck until the lashings are secured.

The trials went very well, and the system worked perfectly. At first it was a very strange sensation to feel the aircraft being manoeuvred and landing without much input from the pilot, but as confidence was built up the advantages of the system could be seen. The disadvantages were the need for the messenger cable to be connected manually, so someone had to be ready out on the deck, and the complexity of the system on the ship. It is interesting that after the Mk. 42A's were completed the 42B's did not have this system fitted, but relied on a free landing, with a Harpoon fitted to the aircraft to secure it after landing, similar to the system in widespread use on the Lynx and Merlin. At the end of the Haul down trials I was asked to give a presentation to the Royal Aeronautical Society in

London. I was very pleased to do this but disappointed when only fifteen people turned up.

To accept the Indian aircraft there was a very strong team from the Indian Navy based at Westlands, including aircrew who flew with us on the acceptance flights. I got to know the leader of the team, Lt. Cdr. Vaidyanathan very well, and the good relationship proved its worth on the many acceptance flights we carried out. Their team was with us for almost five years, and each of their aircraft was meticulously examined and tested before being accepted. The Mk 42A was probably the best anti-submarine helicopter in the world at that time, with the additional role of carrying the long range anti-ship missile, the Sea Eagle. A total of 21 Mk 42B's were delivered, along with six 42C's, which were a simpler troop carrying utility version.

During the development flying there was a requirement for an aircraft to go to the south of France to work on the Mediterranean ranges there. While in the hover it suffered an instantaneous engine run down, and settled gently in to the water. The pilot, John Teasdale, shut down and the crew abandoned the aircraft in to their dinghies. The sea was so calm and warm they barely got wet! Unfortunately after floating for while the aircraft sank in very deep water so the cause was never discovered. This was the only aircraft that ditched during my time at Westlands.

On the production side I was sent frequently to fly brand new Gazelles which had been built at our factory at Weston-super-Mare. This was the old Bristol Aircraft and Helicopter factory where all the Gazelles destined for the British forces were assembled. It still had its own airfield and Air Traffic Control, which was very necessary as it was adjacent to the Bristol Control Zone. This was not particularly popular with the pilots as it was an hour's drive from Yeovil, and a late return, but I enjoyed the trip over the Somerset Levels, and the flying in brand new aircraft. The personnel at Weston took great pride in their work, and we were always made most welcome, with a special Pilot's packed lunch, which included a bottle of beer!

So the production flying and the acceptance of the the Mk 42A Sea Kings kept me pretty busy in the Spring of 1980, but I was about to start on another part of the Test Pilot's job, customer conversions. Inevitably as the company test pilot is the first to become familiar with a new type he becomes the instructor for the first customer pilots. The Lynx had sold widely abroad, and one the first customers was Denmark, with an order for eight Mk.80's. I was given the task of converting four Danish pilots to the aircraft, eight hours each. It was quite a change for them, as their previous aircraft was a much simpler Alouette 3, with no autopilot. I very much enjoyed working with them, but it was a very intensive period, I flew 38 hours in May 1980. We finished the course on time, and the one aircraft we used stayed serviceable for the whole month, which really impressed the customer.

In1980 the Navy decided to form a new Branch of the Royal Navy Reserve, the Air branch. This was to consist of Aircrew who had recently left, to come back for a fortnight every year for refresher flying, so the Navy had an extra pool of experienced aircrew that could be used at short notice. I applied and was accepted to fly the Lynx with 815 Squadron at Yeovilton. This was very valuable to me as it kept me in touch with Naval matters, still one of our prime customers. The firm recognised this, and I was allowed an extra weeks leave, but the second week came out of the four week leave allowance.

In July 1980 I was about to depart on yet another trip to Weston when I was told to stay by the Chief Test Pilot, as he wanted to convert me to the Westland 30.

CHAPTER 14

Westland 30

In the late 1970's it was realised at Westlands that there was a need to develop the Lynx still further, in the hope it would fulfil any future Ministry requirement for a replacement for the Puma and Wessex as well as establishing a foothold in the expanding commercial market. It was decided to use the existing Lynx transmission and rotor, up rated, but with a completely new fuselage and cockpit. The cabin had up to 19 seats, and the power was provided by two Rolls-Royce Gem 41-1 engines, as fitted to the Lynx. This was a private venture, and the first prototype, G-BGHF, first flew in April 1979, just before I joined. I had nothing to do with the project for my first year, until with no prior warning; Roy Moxam took me with him on a short familiarisation flight. Following that I was put straight in to an intensive period of stress measurement. This is a series of flight conditions, and is a major part of the certification process we were seeking with the CAA.

This was the start of my involvement with the Westland 30 for the next eight years, which would include CAA and FAA certification, demonstration flights and many pilot conversions. Much of the development flying I did with a Senior Flight Test Engineer, Malcolm Pester, with whom I had an excellent professional and personal relationship for the next twenty years. As well as bursts of development flying on the Westland 30, I was still doing production flying on the Lynx, Gazelle and Sea King. Also at this time I was being checked out on our new communication aircraft, an Agusta 109, on which I was eventually to become an examiner. It was a period of very mixed and enjoyable flying, which included a period in Denmark checking out the vibration levels on their new aircraft.

It also included my first trip to Paris, ferrying a Sea King for the Paris Air Show. I was part of a three aircraft formation lead by a senior colleague, who got lost over the middle of Paris. We had the mortification of hearing the French controller announcing "There are three Westlands lost over Paris". They sent up another helicopter to guide us in. I then had two further trips to Paris which I managed in the 109.

By now, as well as the test flying I was also helping with the communication flying. The Company had two civilian Gazelles and had recently acquired an Agusta 109 from Agusta, as we started to work closer with the Italian company. I had to carry out a test with a Type Rating Examiner at Fairoaks airfield in Surrey, who turned out to be an ex – colleague from the Navy, Larry Marlow. Most of the comms flights were to the London Heliport owned by Westlands at Battersea.

The next Lynx training was for the Mk. 82 for three Norwegians. Most unusually for a ship borne aircraft it was manned by Air Force pilots The three pilots each had ten hours instruction, and seemed pleased with the aircraft. In service they operated it in some of the extreme conditions off Northern Norway.

Then it was back to the stress programme on the Westland 30, and also the first of many flights with the CAA pilots carrying out their assessments. These were a vital part of Certification, and I was surprised to be trusted with them. The first CAA pilot was Ken Reed, an ex-naval pilot of vast experience, who had been one of the first helicopter pilots in Britain. One of the main points of contention was Pitch runaways. The W30 had a duplex autopilot, which meant a single runaway was opposed by the other good channel, thus little deviation of the aircraft. However the W30 had a strong tendency to pitch up, particularly at aft Centres of Gravities (CG), and some further modification was required. I thus did a lot flying with the manufacturer's representative, Roy Pedley. It was a very intensive period of flying; in September 1981 I flew over 40 hours, mostly in G-BGHF. The next CAA pilot I flew with was Peter Harper, whom I knew from our days in the Navy.

While I was busy with the development flying the first production aircraft, G-BIWY, had flown. This was destined for the first customer, British Airways Helicopters (BAH), to use on the North Sea. WY first flew in September 1981, and joined HF on the development and certification programme. The vital CAA certification was gained in December 1981, and the first two BAH pilots arrived for their conversion to type in January 1982. Needless to say I had been given that job, the first of many. I had been given the Type Rating Examiner qualification by the CAA, without any testing, based on the development flying. Someone has to be first with a new type!

This was the start of a close professional relationship and friendship with Tony Stafford and Les Rose, both very experienced pilots. Tony I had known in the Navy, and we all worked very well together. Whenever a new aircraft is introduced in to service the CAA insist on an intensive period of flying with no passengers, on the routes that will be used. BAH were happy to do this but asked for a manufacturers pilot to help, so I was asked if I was willing to do it. It meant a month away from home, based at Beccles in Suffolk, which is where the aircraft will be based in service.

By coincidence Beccles was my wife's home town, and her recently widowed mother still lived there, so I could live there. I was keen to see the aircraft in service, and also witness North Sea operations, so accepted the challenge. Thus, began in February 1982 a period of very intense flying where we tried to visit all the BAH bases in the UK, ranging from Sumburgh in the north to the Scillies in the south. We also visited a number of rigs in the North Sea, and a trip to Texel in Holland, often flying more than five hours a day. The three of us shared the flying, so I learnt what it was like as a passenger.

This was an ideal opportunity for me to obtain my civil instrument rating, as Les was an Examiner, and needed to be type rated on the W 30, and I could be his student. I had never done this sort of instrument flying before; the military instrument rating was purely the ability to fly solely on instruments, often in a degraded state. The civil rating was mainly procedural, using the radio aids to carry out a self-approach back to an airfield. We made several training flights with Les instructing me, and after ten hours instruction, I took the test with the CAA examiner, and passed! I would never have been able to use the aircraft like that at Yeovil, but I thought a rating may be needed in future dealings with the W30, as it was needed to fly in Controlled Airspace. BAH's headquarters was at Gatwick, so we made several visits there, fitting in with the very busy airliner traffic with no problem. We made many demonstration flights at each BAH base, as all the personnel were eager to see their new acquisition. At the end of the month we had achieved over fifty hours with no defects, and the two BAH pilots were now familiar with the aircraft, and could start training others.

Following my four weeks at Beccles I was now back at Yeovil, but was still flying WY on various tasks, from noise measurement to flying with the FAA pilots.

The FAA certification was particularly important as the potential for sales in the USA seemed very great and a firm based in Los Angeles, Airspur, had decided to lease several aircraft to run a shuttle service from outlying suburban airports to the main international airport.

While I had been away on the North Sea the Falklands campaign had started. Westlands was involved to great extent as many of its aircraft were involved, but its main task was the rapid development of an Air Early Warning (AEW) version of the Sea King, to help protect the fleet from Exocet attacks, which had already proved very costly. This major task which would have taken years normally was achieved in five weeks. My involvement was in the second aircraft which had to be ready to embark on HMS Illustrious, which was sailing for the Falklands on the Monday morning, and it had not yet flown on the previous Friday! We made the initial flight on the Friday evening in terrible weather, and finished the flying over the weekend, just in time to embark on the Monday.

I was a bit concerned with my new role in the Naval reserve I may be called up, but in the event we were not required.

Westlands was keen to expose the W30 as much as possible, so it was entered in the 1982 Farnborough Air

Display, as part of a three aircraft display. WY was lent back to us by BAH, so I flew that daily in the display, as well as several demonstration flights in the evening. Roy Moxam flew the Lynx demonstrator, G-LYNX, in the show, but I did the demonstration flights in the evening, to several foreign customers, none of whom bought the aircraft. This was my second exposure to Farnborough, the previous time with the Naval display sixteen years earlier.

Straight back to Westlands in time for the first flight of the second BIH aircraft, G-BKGD. The main difference between the two aircraft was the cabin door. WY had a sliding door, a hangover from military aircraft, but not liked in the civil world, as it vibrated and was difficult to make draught proof. It was replaced on GD by a two part "stable door", which had a much more positive lock, which became the production standard. I also made three flights with the second FAA pilot which helped achieve FAA certification in December 1982. This was crucial, as the first American operator, Airspur, wished to start pilot training over Christmas.

Before that there was another sales demonstration trip to Scandinavia. This was in GD which had been delivered to BAH, piloted by them on the transits, but by me on the demonstration flights. These were at Rotterdam, Stockholm and Oslo, all big international airports, which required a lot of co-ordination. We managed all the flights successfully, but no orders resulted.

Meanwhile BAH had accepted their third aircraft, G-GOGAS, and another customer, Helicopter Hire, had taken two. The production line was now turning out aircraft for Airspur in Los Angeles, and I found I was to be heavily involved in their operations.

CHAPTER 15

Americal Adventures

Airspur were the first customer in the USA, and was started with the aim of providing a regular service between the many suburban airfields around Los Angeles and the main international airport, LAX. At the time the road traffic to and from LAX was appalling as preparations were being made to expand the airport in anticipation of the forthcoming Olympic Games. It could take an hour to travel the last mile, so a helicopter alternative seemed a good proposition. It was the idea of a local business man, but who was funding the project I never found out. Westlands were desperate to sell the W30, especially in the USA with its own well established helicopter industry.

To fly in the USA I needed an FAA licence, for which I had to appear personally at the local office, which was in Brussels. This I achieved with remarkably little trouble on a day trip, on production of my CAA licence.

For contractual and financial reasons there was a need for the first three aircraft to be accepted at the Airspur base at Long Beach, and the first two pilots converted by 31st December 1982. This meant flying over Christmas, and I was asked to do it. At this time my two boys were five and seven, so it was a great sacrifice to be away, but I had little choice. So I had the first of many ten hour flights to Los Angeles, and met the first two pilots for conversion, Dolph Todd and Burt Rhine, who were the prospective Chief and Deputy Chief pilots. Both were very experienced ex-army pilots, mainly on Huey UH1B aircraft. While we were waiting for the aircraft to be re-assembled by a team from Westlands I was able to run a ground school for the pilots, a job that would normally have been done on a week's course at Yeovil.

I made the first flight with Dolph Todd on Christmas day. As Long Beach, a huge airfield, was busy, we carried out the training at Chino, an airfield about ten miles away, where we caused much local interest. I managed to fly the three aircraft and give the pilots three flights each, including a night flight. It was a revelation for me to fly in the Los Angeles control area, one of the busiest in the world, and already I was wondering how the much slower helicopters were going to fit in.

We were feeling a bit sorry for ourselves, being away from home, my Christmas lunch was a rather stale tuna sandwich! However things improved when one of the Airspur mechanics invited us to their home, to join in their large family party, so I had some turkey after all!

It was obvious that the two pilots were having some difficulty in adapting to the W30, especially to the autopilot, the concept of which was completely foreign to them. The handling of the W30 was completely different to the helicopters they were familiar with. This was the first of many visits to LAX, as every time they had a problem or a complaint I was sent over. I found their operation was struggling, as they were having difficulty fitting in to the extremely busy airliner pattern, and no special arrangements with ATC had been made. Frequently the helicopters were made to hold for 15 minutes or more when the whole trip should only have taken that long. They were also made to carry out a long ground taxi from their landing point on the runway to the gate. Helicopters are not designed to do that, so they soon started to have problems with brakes and tyres.

Meanwhile back in UK BAH were successfully using their three aircraft on the North Sea, and a second operator, Helicopter Hire, had leased two, one of which was fitted with a large external TV camera. The Chief Pilot of Helicopter Hire was another ex- naval friend of mine, Phil Bartley, who was also in the Naval reserve. The conversions in UK all went very smoothly, perhaps because the pilots were much more used to more sophisticated aircraft.

A second customer in the USA, Omniflight, had chosen the W 30 as the ideal aircraft to expand the service they were already operating, a shuttle service between East 60th Street heliport and JFK airport, as a service for Panam First and Club class passengers. The aircraft were painted in Panam colours, and looked very smart. The first three of their pilots came to Yeovil for their conversions which made life much easier for me. They had no trouble converting to the aircraft, which was perfect for that role. Because it was an established operation a special procedure had been developed where the helicopters did not mix with the airliners there was not the same problem that Airspur encountered at LAX, and this popular service ran for four years. It only stopped when Panam hit financial difficulties in 1988.

Before it was shipped to New York it was used for a number of marketing demonstrations in UK, one of which was a demonstration to the Icelandic Coast Guard in Aberdeen. This meant a long trip up the East coast, refuelling at Newcastle. As we were passing the Firth of Forth I looked out to my right and there was a USAF Phantom fighter slowly overtaking us, wondering what on earth a Panam aircraft was doing there! The demonstration went well, but the Icelandic team were never seriously interested.

The day after this long trip (a Saturday) I was sent off to Southend to fly the Helicopter Hire aircraft, G-KATE, with a large television camera mounted on the side. The weather was awful for the drive and the flying but the flying was successful, and we were able to clear the camera for use. The next time I saw it was covering the Boat Race for BB C Television.

The Omniflight aircraft were delivered to Liverpool for shipping across to Newark on a roll on/roll off ship which meant minimum disassembly, and I was invited to fly the aircraft from the docks to the small airfield nearby at Linden where they were based.. I carried out the other conversions there, having checked out their first three pilots at Yeovil some months previously. Their Chief Pilot, Charlie Robinson, came with me on a familiarisation flight round New York, which was surprisingly easy. We flew over the Statue of Liberty and up the East River, where he showed me the East 60th Street heliport, which was the departure point for the shuttle. It was no more than a narrow shelf at the edge of the East river. There was no runway, and the approach and departure were over the river. An engine failure at a crucial time would mean a ditching in the heavily polluted river. That location would never have been permitted in UK, but Omniflight used it for several years.

A third customer had appeared in the USA, Midway Airlines, a large internal airline based in Chicago. Chicago has two major airports; the largest is O'Hare International on the outskirts, and Midway, more central. They planned to use the W30 in the same way as Panam, running a shuttle service between the two airports, thus avoiding a two hour drive. They ordered three aircraft in the company colours which looked very smart. The pilot conversions were carried out in the USA, but I had great difficulty finding a suitable airstrip. Midway airport was far too busy, so we found a small private airstrip, which had been built as part of a proposed development, where each house had its own hangar, and access to the airstrip. The runway was built but nothing else. I was slightly reluctant to use this as obviously there was no fire cover, but I had little choice. It actually worked out very well, the only queries came from some local people who wondered what was going on. We took them for a short flight and everybody was happy.

I converted five of their pilots, and I was rewarded by being taken out to a famous steak restaurant, Chicago being the meat capital of the USA. They insisted I try the fillet, which when it came was the size of our usual Sunday joint! The operation was quite successful, and I went out to them again six months later to take an aircraft to the opening of the new Indianapolis Heliport.

Meanwhile, when I was back at Yeovil I was involved in several demonstration and marketing flights. The most memorable was providing transport for the Head of the Saudi defence forces and his team to various establishments around England, the aim being to demonstrate he aircraft. They were very grateful, but showed little interest in the aircraft. They did present me with a gold watch studded with diamonds, the only present I was given in my entire career.

I also took an aircraft to land in the garden of a very wealthy car dealer in the hope he might buy one. He really took our sales man by surprise when he asked what the price was, and could he get a discount! Westlands was just not used to questions like that. We also gave a demonstration to an American business man who had a huge following in the UK. We took an aircraft to Luton Airport to meet his private jet, and fly him to Cranfield. We were not prepared to see a large crowd of his followers gathered outside the fence at Luton, there just to catch a glimpse of the great man! Again, he was not really interested; he was just using us as handy transport. This was not a market Westlands was good at, they having been mainly a military supplier.

Although at this time I was mainly flying the W30 on Indian production aircraft, I was still flying all the other types in production, the Lynx, Sea King and Gazelle. There was still more development flying on the W 30, particularly on the Autopilot system. I was also back flying a Wasp, after a ten year interval. This was a Royal Navy one, which Westlands had refurbished for the New Zealand Navy. I had no trouble remembering!

While I had been occupied in the States a lot had been going on at Yeovil with selling the W30 to India, culminating in an order for 21 aircraft.

CHAPTER 16

India and the Westland Affair

While I had been away for a lot of 1984/5 my Boss, Roy Moxam, had taken a W30 to India, at the request of their Government, to demonstrate it with a view to using the aircraft to support their emerging off shore Oil and Gas industry. It was also intended to use them for tourist transport in the foot hills of the Himalayas. By some clever negotiation the aircraft were paid for by a Foreign Aid grant from the British Government, so that was indirect support for Westlands. This was sorely needed as the whole W30 private venture had been extremely costly, with little return. The firm was almost bankrupt, and this was brought home to me when I had to fly the Group financial director, Chris Bunker, to Liverpool so he could present a cheque for payment for an Indian Sea King.

The firm had appealed to the Government for help, and a new Chief Executive had been appointed, Sir John Cuckney, who was a specialist in sorting out financial problems like ours. Our relatively small financial problem became a Cabinet issue, in a clash between the Prime Minister, Margaret Thatcher, and the Secretary of State for

Defence, Michael Heseltine. The difference boiled down to the solution of the lack of finance. Heseltine wanted a European solution, with Westlands taken over by British Aerospace and a consortium of European manufacturers. The PM and Cuckney wanted an American solution with Sikorsky providing temporary finance, and a possible arrangement to build Blackhawk helicopters for Saudi Arabia. This was much supported by the Westland Board, as Westlands had been working with Sikorsky for many years. There was such disagreement in Cabinet that eventually Heseltine resigned and walked out. Fortunately for Westlands it was decided the Sikorsky solution was the financial one. If it had gone the other way I think Westlands would have disappeared in a couple of years.

The Indian W30 contract included several pilot conversions. The pilots were all Senior Officers who were coming up to retirement. Although they were helicopter pilots many of them had not flown for some considerable time, so the standard was very variable and they were not very enthusiastic about the aircraft. Fortunately for me, Roy Moxam having been so involved in India, when he retired as Chief Test Pilot took up the job as our representative there. So, he was on the spot to solve any problems. When he retired Trevor Egginton took over as Chief Test Pilot, and I was lucky enough to be promoted to be the Deputy Chief Test Pilot in 1986. From now on my job involved not only the test flying but also the management and running of the department. The flying during this period (1986/7) was very varied, with the run of production W30's, the acceptance of the Indian Sea Kings Mk. 42 B and C, and some development flying on the W30-300.

It was during this period that I suffered the one and only engine failure in my career. I was fortunate that it happened on a twin engine aircraft, a production Westland 30 for India. I was travelling backwards at 30 knots in a very heavy aircraft at a maximum forward CG when one of the engines ran down. I managed to carry out a forward flare and achieve a gentle touch down. I kept the engines running and called for assistance from the Resident Rolls-Royce engineer. Plugging in his diagnostic equipment he found the failure of a potentiometer in the control system, which eventually was modified. My Flight Test Engineer was Dave Gibbings, a man of vast experience who didn't realise what had happened till it was all over!

There was a diversion from this in August 1986 when Westlands was sub contracted by Bond Helicopters to fit a new autopilot to their Aerospatiale 365C aircraft. I was given a quick type conversion by another ex-naval friend, Alan Rock, and we completed the flying in four days, including a check by the CAA pilot. This was necessary for Bond to undertake a contract to support the gas rigs in Morecombe Bay, working from Blackpool. I had to go to Blackpool to check out their pilot, and fly out to the rigs. Seeing the illuminations there was a pleasant conclusion to a very successful trial.

From the early days of the W30 it was obvious the aircraft could be improved by a more powerful and reliable engine, and an increase in weight and speed. This was achieved by fitting the General Electric CT7 engine to a development aircraft, G-FLEC, and to a second G-HAUL. This was a complete re-design, designated the W30-300, with a five bladed rotor, and was much faster and heavier than the original W30-100. It only flew about 50 hours before all development was stopped. If this version had been available earlier, the whole programme might have been more successful. I flew some of the handling development flights on the 30-300, and it felt very different to the standard aircraft, so if the programme had continued there was considerably more development to do.

The W30 programme ended rather prematurely after a series of accidents in India. One was caused by a piece of locking wire which had been left in one of the hydraulic jacks, causing it to lock. Another inexcusably was a tail rotor gearbox failure caused by lack of oil. A third was pilot error when they flew into cloud in a mountainous area and hit the ground. After the third all the W30's in India were grounded. There was nothing wrong with the aircraft, the accidents were the result of poor maintenance and poor piloting.

There had been another accident in the USA in November 1983 when an Airspur aircraft suffered a tail rotor failure at 4000 feet over Los Angeles. By a miracle the aircraft spiralled down completely out of control, and before crashing in one of the very few non built up areas broke through some high tension wires. These must have checked the rate of descent as the six occupants suffered only minor injuries. The cause was the fracture of a control arm in the tail rotor gearbox. All the aircraft were grounded until a solution was found, but as this failure had occurred before on a Royal Navy Lynx Westlands had a solution in hand, by fitting a monitoring system.

However, the big worry was the legal proceedings brought by the pilot concerned against Westlands in a Californian court, as in that State as well as the normal damages the Firm could have also incurred punitive damages, which could have been more than the value of the firm! I was involved as I had done the conversion of the pilot and I had to give evidence in the American court. This was done by three of the Court officials coming over to England and setting up a temporary Court in an hotel in Sherborne. I was concerned that my evidence might involve the Firm but I was massively helped by the Westland legal manager, David Lee, and I did not have to go back to the States. It was eventually settled out of court, and I think Westland got off lightly, as each one of the occupants could have sued for damages. They did not realise it had been a miraculous escape.

I was heavily involved in the W 30 for six years, seeing it through development and production. Forty were built but it was not a success, and nearly broke the Company. I was now moving on to my next Major programme, the EH101.

CHAPTER 17

EH 101 Early Days

When I was at Boscombe Down in the seventies I was involved in writing the specification for the Sea King Replacement, or SKR. After I joined Westlands I found the programme had moved on, and was now a joint programme with Agusta, as the Italian government also needed a replacement for their SH3D's. Before the joint project, in the early 80's Westlands had started their own programme the WG34, and had actually started building a prototype before it was cancelled.

With the support of both Governments a new joint company was formed, European Helicopter Industries (EHI), with a contract to provide an anti-submarine aircraft for both countries. At the same time, it was realised that the same basic airframe could also be used in a civilian and tactical transport version. Thus, a large programme emerged, with nine prototypes and a ground test vehicle, spread between Yeovil and Coscina Costa, near Milan. Design responsibility was split between the two companies, but Westlands had responsibility for the forward fuselage and cockpit, so the test pilot's department became heavily involved in cockpit design. This was particularly interesting for us as it was decided that apart from the first three prototypes, the 101 should have electronic rather than mechanical displays. This was state of the art at the time, with Smiths Industries sub-contracted to provide them. To help develop this, as well as the Autopilot, a full motion Flight simulator was installed at Yeovil. This was a great development tool, as I could "fly" the simulator with the design engineers sitting with me. I spent many hours in the simulator, saving hundreds of expensive flight hours.

Needless to say this was very exciting for me. As a test pilot you are very lucky these days to be involved in a programme from the very beginning through to production and delivery. I had been the project pilot from the beginning, with inputs in to the cockpit design, and attendance at many meetings, some in Italy, the first of many visits to Coscina Costa. The programme evolved in the 1980's, with manufacture of the first two prototypes, PP1 and PP2 commencing in March 1985. These were for basic airframe development, so they had a mechanical cockpit. They were the first of nine prototypes, five in Yeovil and four in Italy.

PP1 was the first to be completed in Yeovil, but the Ground Test Vehicle. (GTV) was running in Italy some time before that. This was a metal frame supporting a complete transmission and three engines, rotor head and blades. It had a cockpit box and as the aim was to complete many hours pulling power, although firmly tied down, it had to be controlled by a pilot. Agusta only had five pilots at the time, so we had to help manning it. This was a chance for us all to get to know each other, and also to become familiar with the aircraft. We spent many hours in the GTV, running late in to the night. It was very reassuring to know the transmission had been tested before the first flight. After a while it became a little boring for the pilot, but it was very necessary, and sending out a Westland pilot to do a spell helped our Italian colleagues.

Before the first flight there was a very lengthy period of ground running on PP1, firstly to check out all the systems on the aircraft, but mainly to check for any signs of Ground Resonance. This is a very dangerous condition for helicopters when an out of balance force at the rotor head acts with the natural frequency of the undercarriage to start a very rapidly increasing "bounce" of the aircraft which can quickly destroy it. Previous trials at Westland had involved fitting heavy tie down cables to the aircraft which could be rapidly tightened in the event of resonance. With the 101 initial calculations showed it should not have any tendency to ground resonance, so it was decided that a very progressive approach to the conditions, with the aircraft being monitored on Telemetry to pick up any tendency. The pilot tried to initiate resonance by "stirring" the cyclic column, starting off at very low rotor revolutions, and gradually increasing them. This was then repeated at a variety of weights and centres of gravity, and undercarriage conditions. The results confirmed the initial calculations, and the 101 had absolutely no tendency to ground resonance, even in the worst conditions. This all took some time, and despite being rolled out in April 1987, PP1 was not ready for the first flight until October. All the ground running had been carried out by Trevor Egginton, the Chief Test Pilot, with me as co-pilot, and we were the crew for the first flight. While being heavily involved in the 101 ground running I was still involved in the other department flying on the Sea King, W 30 and Agusta 109, and also getting used to my new duties as Deputy.

The very first flight of any new aircraft is always a major event, and I was fortunate enough to be involved. Having done so much ground running Trevor and I were now very familiar with the aircraft, and the first flight on October 9th 1987 was planned to be very gentle, with a lift into the hover and some gentle airfield manoeuvres, all being monitored by a team in Telemetry, for us to assess the basic handling. Our back seat crew were two very experienced Flight Test Engineers, Malcolm Pester and Joe Andrewatha. Because the final acceptance work on the simple autopilot had not been finished it had been disconnected, so we had the raw aircraft to assess. It was such a momentous event for Westlands the entire staff were invited to come out on the airfield to witness it, a very rare occurrence. When we were finally ready Trevor lifted off into the hover. Almost immediately the instrumentation monitoring the stress on the tail rotor failed. We could not proceed without this, so we had to land back on after just five minutes. We had been half expecting this as we had had trouble with this in the ground running. It was soon fixed and we were airborne again four days later for some hover manoeuvres on the airfield, which Trevor flew. These were all satisfactory so we were cleared for our first venture in to forward flight.

This could be called the proper first flight, and Trevor was kind enough to let me pilot it, probably the most important flight of my career. It was a great thrill to gently ease the aircraft into a gentle climb, and then hold the speed at 60 knots while we assessed the handling and the vibration levels. I slowly increased speed up to 80 knots, and then up to a 100, the maximum we were permitted. Trevor and I had had high hopes for the vibration levels, as we had the new rotor blades fitted. We looked at each other. The vibration levels were already high, and would obviously increase with speed. These were the 5R high frequency vibrations, the basic frequency of the airframe, not the blades. The handling was fine, and everything else on the aircraft was working perfectly. After 25 minutes we landed back and faced the intensive debrief. This was the start of the intensive programme to reduce the vibration, which eventually resulted in a major design change. After four more short flights to gather more data, PP1 was laid up for three months. Meanwhile in Italy PP2 had its first flight in November 1987. Trevor went out to participate with Raf Longobardi, the Agusta Chief Test Pilot.

During this period in March 1988 I was promoted to Chief Test Pilot, with the prospect of holding that position for at least 11 years. It was a great compliment and justified my decision to leave the Navy nine years before. The prospects for Westlands were now looking good after the Heseltine affair, with the huge EH 101 programme, and the prospect of several other large Ministry programmes to come. I took over a department of ten test pilots, all individuals, and ex-service. I also had responsibility for Air Traffic Control, Safety Equipment and became the Airfield Manager. When I took over I was responsible to the Engineering Director, Richard Case, who was an old friend of mine. I was not happy with this arrangement, as it could lead to a clash over key technical decisions. Fortunately, I was able to change this so I became directly responsible to the Managing Director, John Varde. Although not a Director I attended Board meetings, which was just the level that suited me.

I had been friends with some of the pilots for several years, in fact Stuart Collins had been my best man 15 years before, but the relationship now had to change. I got off to a good start with the pilots as I arranged a pay increase and incorporation back on to the Company car scheme. All the pilots were very experienced, and some had joined the Company some years before me, but there was no problem in accepting my appointment.

I was also entitled to a Secretary, an important job as I was often flying and dealing with a high level of people in the MOD and CAA. I was lucky enough to find Caron Martinez who stayed with me for several years, and was a great support particularly on those difficult days that happen sometimes. She was so good she became the Managing Director's secretary! Her replacement was Michelle Jeffrey who was equally efficient, who stayed with me until I retired. We must have got on well, as she entered me for a Boss of the year competition in a magazine. We came second, but I was the envy of all the other Directors!

I also had to start my relationship with the Director of Flying MOD PE, who was my direct boss in the Ministry, who had the responsibility for most of the military aircraft we flew, as well as approving all the pilots, including myself. The post was held by an RAF Group Captain at Boscombe Down, with a staff to support him. I also had to have a similar relationship with the CAA Flight Test department, as the 101 was also going to have civil certification. There was a lot to learn, as well as budgets to maintain.

I needed a Deputy, and I chose Derek Marpole, an ex-Army pilot with whom I had served at Boscombe Down. As well as taking on my new responsibilities, I was now leading the flying on PP1, as Trevor had retired. We were now expanding the flight envelope, and I was introducing other pilots to the aircraft. All development flying had to stop as the aircraft was being prepared for its first public appearance at Farnborough in September 1988.

This was going to be the first public appearance of the 101, so obviously I had to fly it. At the same time it was decided we should have a combined Westland display, incorporating a Lynx ant two Blackhawks, one of ours and one from Rolls-Royce. Theirs was fitted was fitted with the new RTM 322 engines, which they hoped the MOD would choose to be fitted to all the British aircraft. This was a very busy Farnborough for me, as I was displaying a priceless prototype, was responsible for the Westland display, and was a member of the Flying Control Committee (FCC) for the first time. This was a duty that came with the job, the FCC supervised the flying display and consisted of all the CTP's from the British aviation industry.

I was very limited as to what I could do in my display, but I was very glad to be accompanied by Raf Longobardi, the Agusta CTP on all the display flights, and we became firm friends. The display went down well, and the MOD announced that all the UK 101's would be fitted with the RTM engine, which was great news for Rolls Royce. Farnborough, though very necessary, caused a lengthy interrupt to the development programme. By the end of the first 50 hours on PP! and PP2 we had covered the flight envelope up to the maximum speed, altitude and weight, with no handling problems, and the aircraft had been assessed by the civil and military testing agencies. However the flying rate was rather slow, and it was decided to base both prototypes in Italy, as there was a better weather factor there. This meant a large team from Westlands being detached there for up to two years, including a pilot. Derek Marpole volunteered for this, so Jerry Tracey became Deputy temporarily. PP1 was shipped out to Italy, and spent the next two years there working with PP2 on basic airframe development.

Meanwhile the programme continued to expand with the first flight of PP3 in September 1988. PP3 was the first aircraft in the civil form, and had up rated CT7 engines. It was carrying on the basic airframe clearance, including the first look at the new autopilot, and the measurement of the pitot and static system, using the trailing bomb method. The vibration levels on PP3 were much the same as PP1, which showed the urgent need to solve this. A temporary fit was a vibration absorber fitted the rotor head. This had worked on the Lynx, but was only partially successful on the 101.

The solution was a radically new system called Active Control of Structural Response (ACSR). This was the replacement of the struts holding the main rotor gearbox in place with large hydraulic actuators. These were controlled by signals from a micro-processor, responding to signals from several accelerometers measuring the vibration. Effectively the vibration was being cancelled at source. Much of the development work was done on PP3, and the improvement was dramatic. The pilot now had a vibration ON/OFF switch in the cockpit.

The next aircraft to fly, in June 1989, was PP4 which was the first avionic development prototype, with a full electronic cockpit and navigation systems. The development programme was now in full swing, with four aircraft, and the flying was now spread to the other test pilots. This aircraft was chosen to be the first to be fitted with the RTM 322 engines, so after the initial navigation and autopilot assessments it was withdrawn for the engine fit. Its place was taken in October 1989 by PP5, the first Naval version. This was fitted with the radar and sonic systems, all working on the first flight.

The Royal Navy had initially ordered the aircraft with the sonics system as the submarine detection system, which involved dropping and monitoring sonobuoys. When it was realised that they were not good enough to track the new Russian submarines the specification was changed to incorporate a new dipping sonar. This was more powerful than any previous system, and was a major design change. The Italian naval aircraft was always going to be fitted with a dipping sonar, a different one to the British fit.

PP7 was the first Utility version with a rear ramp, and PP8 was the first full civil variant which flew in Yeovil in April 1990. As well as the intensive development programme there were many demonstration flights, including one with the First Sea Lord. I also flew the then Chief of Defence Procurement, Peter Levene, who was obviously checking on one of his major projects. Although we were nearly three years in to development, we still didn't have the production contract.

CHAPTER 18

Merlin in production

One of the handling problems we encountered early on was an uncommanded pitch up just as the aircraft comes in to the hover. There was plenty of control to overcome it, but it was an unpleasant feature, especially when coming into the hover alongside a ship prior to landing. After much investigation it turned out the culprit was the large symmetrical horizontal stabiliser, fitted beneath the tail cone. The downwash from the rotor was pushing the tail down as it passed over the stabiliser during the transition. The stabiliser is necessary on all helicopters to improve pitch stability in forward flight. The pitch up has been a common problem on many helicopters, and manufacturers have found different ways of dealing with it. On the Sikorsky Blackhawk the whole stabiliser is tilted as the aircraft slows down. The problem was acute on the 101 because the downwash is so strong and concentrated.

Several solutions were tried. First the stabiliser was removed, which solved the problem, but the pitch stability in forward flight was badly affected. We then tried a much smaller stabiliser, but surprisingly the problem still occurred. We then tried a Sea King stabiliser, high set, just on the right side. This worked well, but would not allow the tail to fold. The final answer was a large asymmetric stabiliser mounted low on the right side. When folded it tucked under the rear fuselage.

Raf and I decided the best way to prove this was a solution was to try some deck landings on a frigate. The official deck landing trial in UK was not due for some time, so Raf organised unofficially an Italian frigate, the Maestrale, which was captained by a friend of his. We used PP2 working from the Italian naval airfield at Luni, on the west coast of Italy, and were able to make the approaches in the different configurations. We were only supposed to hover alongside assessing the pitch up, but it was so calm we decided to land on, and so carried out the first deck landings. It was only once we got out to the ship we found it was actually their Families' day, and the deck was covered with spectators! Only in Italy could this happen. These impromptu deck trials took place in July 1990, six months before the official integration trials on HMS Norfolk, the first of the type 23 frigates, the first ships designed to accommodate the EH 101/Merlin. The integration trials did not include the operating trials, for the first landings the ship was at anchor. The aircraft was folded and stowed in the hangar using the deck handling system, a vital part of the ship aircraft interface with such a large aircraft.

By the end of 1990 the eight prototypes had flown 850 hours of the 4000 planned development hours, but still no production contract. The reason for this was reluctance by the two governments to give such a large contract to two companies whose value was less than the value of the contract. They wanted a prime contractor who was large enough financially, and who would be responsible for risk taking and systems performance. Westlands teamed with the giant IBM company, and at last the production order was signed in September 1991. The order was for 44 Merlin HM1's in the ASW role for the Royal Navy, and 22 Utility variants for the Royal Air Force. The Italian Navy had a requirement for 42 aircraft, and there had been a lot of interest from foreign customers, particularly Canada.

Canada needed a replacement for its very old Sea King ASW aircraft, and stated a requirement for 45 aircraft. A separate Company was formed in Canada, and the aircraft were going to be assembled there. However, in 1993 there was a change of government, and the order was cancelled, which was a great disappointment. Having failed to find a suitable replacement for the SAR requirement, in1998 Canada came back with an order for15 aircraft in the SAR role. These aircraft were to be built in Italy and self ferried to Canada across the Atlantic. Japan, Portugal and Denmark had also expressed an interest in the SAR version and with work proceeding on the Civil certification the future was looking bright for the EH 101.

1991 was a very busy year, with PP5 carrying out trials of the operational systems, PP4 developing the new RTM engines, and PP1 & 3 continuing the certification work. PP8 was now joining in this work, as well as flying on many demonstrations. PP1 had now returned to Yeovil, having self ferried across the Alps, and was now involved in developing a cure for the "Shuffle", a low frequency lateral vibration caused by turbulence from the main rotor head hitting the tail pylon. This long standing feature was eventually cured by modifications to the shape of the engine cowlings, and a large circular fairing on the rotor head itself. PP3 was pursuing the certification requirements, which included high altitude hovering. This was very difficult, as we had to be certain we were in the true hover with no external references. Various methods were tried, including firing a smoke puff from the aircraft and trying to hover alongside it, not very successfully. When we got back I had a phone call from a very worried gentleman who was concerned that someone was trying to shoot us down, as we seemed to be surrounded by anti-aircraft fire! The information was finally obtained in Italy, as there are some handy mountains close to Coscina Costa.

Two production lines were set up, one in Yeovil and one in Coscina Costa. Major components were made in both countries and transported by road, and the programme seemed well under way. There was a lot of other flying going on of course, including two special ones. One was a trip in the A 109 for the Duchess of Kent from London to Taunton where she was visiting a school. She was absolutely charming and borrowed a map so she could follow our progress. The other was a flight out to HMS Ark Royal with the first Sea Lord, Sir Julian Oswald, who was hosting his French opposite number and was showing off his new kit. The French of course had nothing like the Merlin so he didn't say much. I knew Sir Julian from my time in the Naval Reserve, and I think they were both impressed with the new technology.

1992 was also very busy at Yeovil with PP 1, 3,4, 5 & 8 all flying on development tasks, looking towards civil certification. For the first time we were trying to achieve this simultaneously with the CAA, FAA and the European authorities. PP8 took part in the Farnborough air display, and Raf Longobardi came over for couple of days, to fly with me on a couple of the displays.

One of the many demonstrations we gave was to Michael Heseltine, now Minister for Trade and industry, some 7 years after his infamous involvement in Westlands I mentioned earlier. All was now congratulations for us, and he dealt very easily with the many aggressive questions from the large gathering of the press when we landed.

In December the deck trials continued with PP5 on HMS Iron Duke, a brand new Type 23 frigate. This time the emphasis was on the flying, with the intention of proving the aircraft's suitability to operate from a frigate, as there had been some scepticism in the Navy. The manufacturer is not normally involved in this type of trial, it is the responsibility of Boscombe, as I had done when I was there. It was the first deck landings I had done for some time, so I approached them very cautiously. Like the Lynx the Merlin had a harpoon to attach it to the grid after landing. This was the first time it had been used in anger on a moving ship, although many hundreds had been carried out on test rigs ashore. We had been some time into the trial when I had just landed and engaged the harpoon when the ship rolled as it turned. The head of the harpoon snapped off, leaving me with no attachment to the ship, which was still manoeuvring. I thought it best to immediately take off before I slipped off, and returned to Yeovil. It turned out that only a certain amount of angular movement of the harpoon had been expected, and when this was exceeded on board, the head snapped off. When more movement was permitted the problem was solved. It showed however many trials you carry out ashore there is no substitute for taking a Naval aircraft to sea.

Another similar problem that appeared two days in to the trial was the build up of metal chips in the main gearbox. All the gearboxes in the aircraft have chip detectors which warn of unusual wear, and bring up a warning in the cockpit. This gearbox had no history of any excessive wear, so it was obviously something to do with the deck operations. I called a halt to the trial and took the aircraft back to Yeovil for investigation. It turned out the wear was caused by the vertical shock which occurred when the harpoon is released, causing a slight movement of the gears.

The whole trial had gone well, we carried out 67 landings with various wind speeds and directions, and proved conclusively the Merlin was perfectly suited to small ship operations. However, the programme was about to be hit by a devastating accident.

❁

CHAPTER 19

Disaster

On 21st January 1993 I was attending a progress meeting at Yeovil with MOD officials, one of whom Simon Thornewill, was an old friend from my time in the Navy, when a message came from Italy that PP2 had crashed in flames. This devastating news was then made worse when we learned all four aircrew had perished, including my friend and colleague Raf Longobardi, my opposite number at Agusta. This of course put a halt to all EH 101/ Merlin flying while the cause was established. As the aircraft was fully instrumented and had an Accident Data Recorder the cause was soon established. The very powerful rotor brake had somehow come on in flight, overheated and started a fierce fire in the area above the cockpit. This area is a mass of control rods and hydraulic pipes and components. The control rods were made of composite material for lightness, and must soon have burnt through, giving Raf no chance of control at all.

Rotor brakes are an important feature of any naval helicopter, as there is a need to rapidly slow the rotor on shutdown, or the blades can "sail" in any strong wind, and can dip down to waist height at the front of the disc, depending on the stiffness of the blade. It is also a key part of the automatic blade fold system, as the rotor head must be locked in the correct position before folding. The brake also holds the rotor stationary against an engine running on starting, but only when the engine is at ground idle. It is normally a simple system, like a car braking system, with a metal disc and brake pads. It is obvious that the system only operates for a few seconds on shut down, but must not come on in flight as the heat generated will rapidly cause a fire. Several helicopters have been lost because the rotor brake came on in flight, either inadvertently, or because of a fault.

The EH 101 rotor brake was unusual in that it had carbon discs and carbon pads, like a Concorde wheel brake. This system can cope with much higher temperatures, and was incorporated as the rotor disc is quite heavy, and there was a specification requirement to stop the rotor against an engine running at ground idle. The reason for this I never did discover, as I could never imagine an operational requirement to do this. The end result was a very powerful brake, with a complex hydraulic control system, which for some reason on PP2 came on in flight.

The accident and the loss of four crew had an enormous effect on both Companies. Westlands had not lost any aircrew since the fixed wing days of the fifties, and Agusta had never lost any at all. It brought home to all the Flight Test Aircrew at Westlands the risks of our job, and there was a reason for the extra flying pay. I called a meeting the next day, and invited everyone to think about their job, and whether they still wanted to continue. All the pilots, being ex-service had encountered the loss of a colleague at some point, but for the younger Flight Test Engineers it was the first time, and they needed the reassurance and encouragement to continue, particularly flying in the EH 101 again.

The effect on the Agusta aircrew was inevitably deeper, as they had lost their close friend and leader. Accompanied by some of the most senior Westland management we flew out in an executive jet to Coscina Costa for the mass funeral. The funeral was held in the large church in the local town of Gallarate, and it seemed as if the whole town and Agusta workforce was there. I was surprised at the pessimistic mental state of the Agusta pilots, and could see they would need a good deal of encouragement to fly again in the 101, particularly as there seemed to be no hurry to appoint a new Chief Test Pilot.

When the cause had been established a complete redesign of the rotor brake system was started. This included putting the discs and pads in a fire proof box, and most crucially including a clutch system which disconnected the rotor brake from the transmission once the rotor was engaged. There was also a complete design review of the whole aircraft from a safety point of view, which resulted in some major modifications. For example, the composite control rods were replaced by stainless steel ones.

All this took some time, and the aircraft were not cleared to fly again for a period of seven months. During this period other flying continued, mainly on the new Lynx 9, a wheeled version for the Army, and the Mk. 95 a Naval variant for Portugal. I was busy attending many design meetings, which were intended to re-assure me and all the aircrew on the safety and integrity of the 101. I also spent some time in Italy with the Agusta pilots, who were gradually getting over their loss, but still had not appointed a new Chief Test Pilot.

PP4 was the first aircraft to be ready shortly followed by PP5 and PP1. I made the first flight on all of these, and we then started an intensive period of trials flying on all these aircraft, and I had no objections from any of the aircrew. PP8 joined in later, so we had four prototypes flying at the same time, all carrying out development flying. As well as this we had several VIP demos, one of which was to the Prime Minister, John Major. He had requested a flight so we organised one for him in PP5, which was the naval version representative of the version ordered by his government. Because of an old knee injury, he had some difficulty with the aircraft steps, so we had to shut down for him to embark. Once we were airborne he surprised me by asking what was the main purpose of the aircraft! He obviously hadn't been briefed, or had forgotten it. He showed a keen interest, which paid off a few months later when we flew him and the German Chancellor Kohl to Chequers.

PP4 was busy with the new RTM 322 engines which were fitted for the first time, and I was pleased when Ken Robertson, the Chief Test Pilot of Rolls Royce came to fly with us. It was also carrying out AFCS development, in particular the automatic transition into the hover. The EH101/Merlin had two methods of detecting a submarine, Sonics where a number of small sonobuoys are dropped from altitude, and Sonar where a large complex array is lowered in to the water from the hover. There is thus a need for the Autopilot to rapidly bring the aircraft down from altitude to a lower cruise level, and from there into the hover. This had never been achieved before so there was a lot of development flying, even though we had spent many hours in the simulator developing profiles. The manufacturer, Smith's Industries, had a representative at Yeovil, Ken Potter, who had no experience of helicopters but flew with us on all the flights, where he rapidly saw what was needed, and we had an excellent working relationship.

The trip to Chequers I have described in Appendix 1 "A Brush with Fame".

PP8, the civil variant, was very busy carrying out Civil Certification flying. This included flying with the CAA test pilot, Nigel Talbot. We had known each other for a long time, and so far had found nothing that would prevent this. Some years later Nigel finished up working for Agusta! The pressure on the programme was so great that we even flew for three days over the 1994 Christmas break.

We started the third deck trial on HMS Northumberland in March 1995, and this time we stayed on the ship for three days and carried out 40 deck landings as well as checking the ship interfaces. We started to establish a deck landing envelope, in the knowledge that in due course Boscombe would carry out the full release trials. We were more interested in ensuring the problems we had encountered on the previous trials had been overcome, particularly the harpoon, and indeed they had. This was also an opportunity for two other of my ex-Navy test pilots, Nigel Mags and Roger Mowbray, to carry out some landings to make sure it was not just my opinion how the aircraft was suitable for small ship operations. In due course once the Merlin was in service these became routine.

The Northumberland trials were a great success, but our confidence in the aircraft was about to be shaken a second time, this time much closer to home.

CHAPTER 20

Disaster 2

On Friday April 7th 1995 I was airborne in PP8 carrying out routine noise measurement when Air Traffic called me to say PP4 had crashed near Honiton, and three parachutes had been seen. This was terrible news, as I knew there had been four people on board. Jon Dickens and Don Maclaine were the pilots, and Alistair Wood and Geof Douthwaite were the Flight Test Engineers in the back. As we were already airborne we flew over to the site to find where the aircrew were. We found the wreckage of PP4 in a farmer's field and shortly after a Land Rover arrived with Don, Geof and Alistair on board all clutching their parachutes. They had all been picked up by a local farmer, and were shaken but unhurt. The best news was that Jon had left it very late before baling out, and his chute had just opened before he hit the ground. He was injured but had already been picked up by the Devon Helimed helicopter and was on his way to Exeter Hospital. There was nothing else I could do there so I flew the other three back to Yeovil. I was particularly careful, as I was badly shaken by this second accident, and made sure Ted Mustard, who was my co-pilot monitored what I was doing. I sent the three survivors down to the medical centre to be checked out, and tried to find out from the hospital how Jon was. The good news was he had a badly wrenched knee, but otherwise was unhurt. He would be kept in overnight.

Back at Yeovil I had the difficult task of informing the appropriate authorities on a Friday afternoon. PP4 was a military aircraft so there had to be a military Board of enquiry, helped by experts from the Accidents Investigation Board. I also had to organise security of the crash site from Westlands own security staff, not easy on Friday afternoon to cover the weekend. I also had to start our own investigation into what had happened by talking to the aircrew. Next morning, I drove down to Exeter to find Jon had been released and had gone home! This was really good news, so I could telephone him to get his account.

The flight was to check engine handling at altitude, in this case 12000 feet. We very rarely fly at such high altitudes, and the MOD rules are that parachutes are to be worn on any test flights over 3000 feet. This is generally unpopular as they are uncomfortable over long periods. However, I had always insisted the rule was obeyed, very fortunately in this case. Baling out from a helicopter was virtually unknown, as we normally operate at low altitudes where there wouldn't be time to open a chute. It was little short of miraculous that the failure occurred on this particular flight as if it had happened on any of the many previous ones the result would have been fatal. Of course, I had flown PP4 frequently, including several VVIP demonstrations, so the accident was very sobering for me personally, and I was very thankful that I had not lost any of the aircrew under my care.

So what had happened? How could there have been another major failure, especially after such a careful safety audit after PP2's accident. I went around to debrief Jon who was recovering at home. It seemed he was just settling at 12000 feet and slowing down when the aircraft suddenly started to spin rapidly to the left, as if he had applied full left rudder. The other aircrew recognised control had been lost and bailed out without waiting for further instructions, and fell clear before opening their chutes. Jon as Captain recognising a tail rotor malfunction tried to start the correct procedure for dealing with it. He was probably one of the most skilled and experienced helicopter pilots in the country and could not believe he could not cope with the situation. His attention was drawn to his rapidly unwinding altimeter when one of his pencils was pulled from his kneepad and lay across the altimeter. He decided it was time to go, but as he left the aircraft his knee got stuck by the instrument panel, and was damaged when he wrenched it free. He managed to open his chute just before he hit the ground, with seconds to spare. It was a very close call indeed. It was not surprising that Jon chose never to fly in helicopters again and activated the very generous Loss of Licence/Approval insurance which covered all the test pilots.

On the Monday morning following the accident I gathered all the aircrew together, pilots and Flight Test Engineers. I discussed the cause and the need for us all to think about our job and its hazards, and what actions were taken before we were happy to fly in the EH101 again. I finished by thanking George Bain, our one and only Safety Equipment worker who always worked quietly away in his workshop. Because George had done his job properly over many years four of our colleagues were alive today. George, who was in the room, burst in to tears!

I flew over the crash site on the Sunday morning to take some photographs. As well as the fortunate escapes we had been very lucky the crash had occurred in open country side, which vindicated our policy of always carrying out test flying over such areas. Nevertheless the crash site was not far from the very busy A303 or the large farmhouse where the owner of the field lived. He was very helpful throughout, and he was fully compensated for the loss of the use of his field for a couple of years, as it was badly contaminated by composite material, which was widely used in manufacturing. While I was there I met the Accident Investigator who was already on site picking over the wreckage. It was obvious there had been a tail rotor control failure, but where and why had it occurred. Analysis of the Accident Data Recorder showed that full tail rotor pitch had been applied at the tail rotor gearbox, but with no movement of the pedals in the cockpit, which showed the break must have occurred in one of the several composite rods which linked the pedals to the tail rotor. This was puzzling as the rods were virtually unbreakable. The culprit was soon discovered, it was the long one piece rod which ran up the front of the tail fin, the longest rod in the chain. The rod hadn't broken but the metal fitting which connected the rod to the bell crank had fractured, probably caused by vibration induced fatigue. The weight of the rod caused it to fall downwards, applying full tail rotor pitch. The problem of vibration in this rod had been anticipated on design, and a detuning weight should have been attached to the rod. This was not fitted to PP4, and it was discovered that the same part number had been assigned to the rod, with or without the weight. This must have happened a long way back in the design/supply chain, and showed the smallest of errors can have a disastrous effect in aviation.

The aircraft were all grounded again for about three months while a design solution was found. This was a strong spring fitted to the tail rotor control in the gearbox, which in the event of a control fracture would force the tail rotor pitch to a neutral position. The aircraft remains controllable for a running landing. As the cause was quickly established and a modification designed and fitted we were airborne again after three months. I made the first flight again in PP3 to check the proposed running landing technique was viable. It was, and then became a standard part of the training. The Merlin/101 programme then resumed with PP3 and 5, but by this time (August 1996) the production line was well underway.

The first Naval production aircraft RN 01 ZH821 first flew on December 6th 1995. This was a momentous occasion for Westlands and yet again all personnel were invited up to the airfield to watch, so there was a huge crowd to watch me lift off. The flight went perfectly, so all the many changes that had been incorporated from the development programme were proved. It had been eight years from the first flight of PP1, and although it looked similar RN01 was very different. This was the start of 44 aircraft for the Royal Navy, and 22 for the Royal Air Force.

This was not the end of the tail rotor saga as in August 1996 PP7 suffered another tail rotor control failure, this time of the long control rod within the tail rotor gearbox. The spring could not help in this case as it was in the control system before the gearbox. However the tail rotor went to a nominally neutral pitch giving Bruno Bellucci some control as long as he maintained forward airspeed. This made a fast running landing inevitable, which he attempted on the long runway at Malpensa airport. Bruno did a magnificent job but the aircraft turned on its side in the ensuing landing. The airframe was badly damaged, but was rebuilt and flew again. Very fortunately the aircrew were uninjured. The rod which broke was strengthened, and there were no further problems.

Once RN01 was finally completed it became a trials aircraft to prove the production standard was acceptable, while development flying was still continuing on PP3,5 and 8. It appeared at Farnborough in September 1996, where I was a member of the Flying Control Committee. The second production aircraft, RN02 had its first flight in January 1997 and after that there was a fairly regular output. The time had come to start preparing the customer for the introduction of the Merlin.

CHAPTER 21

Merlin into Service

Although the Merlin development took a very long time, eleven years from first flight to first delivery to the RN, it was a very large and complex programme, and there had been several delays during development. There were 44 Royal Naval aircraft to be built, and the last one, RN 44 ZH 864, was delivered to Culdrose in December 2002. The first four continued development flying, including the first icing/snow trial at Uplands, in Ottawa, the same base I had been carrying out the same trials over 20 years ago.

The Navy decided they needed to carry an intensive operational assessment of the aircraft at the Autec range in the Bahamas using Service aircrew. The problem was the aircraft had not yet achieved its Certificate of Airworthiness (C.A.Release) so it could not be flown by them, only by MOD test pilots. The rather unique solution was for the flying and the aircrew to come under my supervision. I was quite happy to accept this, as I knew the pilots involved, and it was the only way for the trials to go ahead The three aircraft involved, PP5 , RN 2 and 3, were shipped out to Florida, and the trial was a great success lead by a friend of mine, Lt. Cdr. Al Howden. It was very gratifying to see the aircraft performing the task it had been designed for.

There were a number of VIP demonstrations in this period, including the Chief of the Air Staff, and the Duke of York at that time a Lynx pilot in the Navy. He was very interested in the new aircraft, and was very polite and deferential, not at all like his reputation that preceded him.

As well as the production flying of the new aircraft there was a very intensive period of flying on RN1, including the load survey which was a comprehensive measurement of all the stresses on the production aircraft. PP3 and PP5 were still carrying out trials, so 1998 was a very busy year for us. We also had a visit of PP7 from Italy flown by my good friend Fabio Frisi, who had been eventually appointed as Chief Test Pilot at Agusta. PP9 also visited for the Farnborough Air Show, and their presence allowed us to have the one and only six aircraft formation of development EH101's! I had become more involved in the Flying Control Committee so for the 1998 show I was happy not to be flying, but supervising instead. It had been ten years since I first demonstrated PP1 there.

While attention had been concentrated on the Naval version, both British and Italian, the RAF aircraft had started construction on the production line. The RAF had been rather reluctant customers for the Merlin, regarding it as primarily a Naval aircraft; they would rather have had more Chinooks. I decided we needed an ex-RAF test pilot at Westlands to help with acceptance, and was lucky enough to employ Andy Strachan, an ex-Chinook instructor. Andy was a very professional aviator, and highly regarded in the RAF. The decision was a wise one, and Andy helped enormously in getting the aircraft accepted. It eventually served for three years in Afghanistan in the most demanding conditions. Andy and I made the first flight of the RAF version (ZJ 117) on Christmas Eve 1998, by which time we were up to the tenth RN Merlin, and we had started delivery to Culdrose, where the first squadrons were forming.

June 10th 1999 was a crucial date for me, my 55th birthday, and my original retirement date when I joined Westlands. However the MOD rules had changed and it was now possible to continue flying beyond the age of 55. We were now in the middle of the Merlin delivery programme, as well as some continuing development flying, so I was asked by my Boss, Richard Case, to consider staying on for a period as Chief Test Pilot. This would mean leaving the Firm on Friday, and starting again with a new contract on Monday. I was quite happy to do this, as I still very much enjoyed the challenge of test flying and was not yet ready to retire. Another factor was the lack of an obvious successor, as Jerry Tracey, who had been the Deputy Chief Test Pilot for some time developed an unexpected medical problem, and was grounded. I promoted Don Maclaine, an ex-Army pilot I had recruited some years previously for the huge Apache programme, of which more later. It was agreed I should stay on for a few more years as Chief Test Pilot, and then remain part time to fly the Export Lynx, and eventually act as the Communications Pilot on the Company A109. This suited me perfectly, a gradual run down to retirement. The next three years I was very happy flying production test flying on the Mk. 1 and 3 Merlin, and on the up rated Lynx for Germany, Korea, Malaysia and Oman.

Meanwhile, away from Yeovil, as part of the military reliability trial PP8 & 9 had been detached to intensively fly 6000 hours over a three year period. For half of this time they were based at Brindisi in Italy, where Agusta had a factory, and half at Aberdeen. We did not have the aircrew to support this, so the whole operation was sub-contracted to Bristow's, who were very interested in the civil version. The arrangement worked very well, and the 6000 hours were accomplished safely, with no reliability problems, flying representative profiles. One exceptional trip was the first Trans Atlantic crossing, via Iceland, Greenland and Northern Canada in August 1999. This was for PP9 to appear at various Air Shows in Canada, after the aircraft was finally ordered in the SAR version, despite previous cancelations. As all the aircraft were to be self ferried from Italy to Canada this was an excellent proving flight.

CHAPTER 22

VVIP Demonstrations

In July 2000 Westlands had a request from 10 Downing Street to fly the Prime Minister and his party from London to Exeter to attend a party conference. As it was a Labour party event he could not use government aircraft, and by flying there and back in one day (a Saturday) it saved him a lot of time. Westlands of course, so dependent on Government orders, was happy to help, so on Saturday July 8th I flew PP8 from Yeovil to Battersea to pick up Tony Blair. Thank goodness it was a glorious day so there were no weather problems. On the way down the PM came up to talk to us. He was very pleasant and interested in the aircraft, and grateful for the ride. It so happened that this was the day after his son was found in the gutter having had too much to drink. Having two teenage sons myself I told him there probably not a father in the country that didn't sympathize with him.

We landed at Exeter University, and the PM was whisked away past a very noisy pro-hunting demonstration. The aircraft was guarded by the local police during his absence, who were fascinated by our large aircraft, with 30 seats.

The return flight to Battersea had more passengers than the downward flight as more of the PM's staff took advantage of the rapid return, and we had plenty of spare seats. The PM was very grateful, particularly as arriving by helicopter he avoided the demonstration.

In March 2001 HRH Prince Philip was invited to visit Westlands, mainly to unveil a memorial created by the Apprentices, but really to give him a flight in an Apache. No member of the Royal Family had done this, and as an ex-helicopter pilot he was determined to be the first. It was also a chance for us to demonstrate the Civilian EH101, by using PP8 to ferry him down from London. The101 was too big to land in the gardens of Buckingham Palace, so we were permitted to use Wellington Barracks, just next door. The parade ground at the Barracks is long and narrow, with an approach over Saint James' park from the river. We had landed PP8 there some years previously, with Prime Minister John Major, and Chancellor Kohl, so I was familiar with it, but it was not an easy approach, and essential not to overshoot, as there were buildings at the end.

We had been in touch with the CO of the Royal Flight and ascertained the Prince would prefer to fly in the cockpit for the trip down, so I shut down the aircraft at the Barracks to await his arrival. He arrived on time, and remarked how noisy the aircraft sounded in the Palace! He had no trouble getting in to the left hand seat, despite the fact he was well into his seventies. Although it was a Royal Flight we had no particular priority, so I made sure to keep a good look out. Halfway down another Royal helicopter crossed our track in front of us with Princess Anne on board. That would have been a near miss to avoid!

He was interested in the new electronic instrument panel, and enjoyed the scenery we passed, particularly

Sherborne Abbey which he had recently visited with the Queen. We landed at Yeovil exactly on time to be met by various Westland and local dignitaries, who took him away for the unveiling. An hour later he was back for his Apache flight. He was being piloted by Don Maclaine, an ex-Army pilot who I had recruited for the Apache programme. The Apache front cockpit is quite difficult to get in to, so the Duke had to change in to a brand new set of flying overalls, which he did in my office. My secretary, Michelle, was so thrilled to meet him, she nearly curtsied!

The short flight to Merryfield went well, but we were all very relieved when he came safely back, having enjoyed his flight. A Royal Fight helicopter came to pick him up and fly him to Sandringham.

In December 1989 the Royal Flight was seeking a replacement for their venerable Wessex. Westlands suggested a version of the S61 Blackhawk of which we had a demonstration model sold to us by Sikorsky after the Heseltine affair. The Prince of Wales was visiting a farm belonging to the Duchy of Cornwall in the local area, but was then going back to Highgrove via Kemble airfield so it was suggested we flew him in the Blackhawk. I was not qualified in the Blackhawk, so I gave the task to John Dickens, our very well qualified instructor. The pickup was at 1530 so most of the flight would be at night. I took the co-pilots seat from Yeovil to the farm, and then travelled in the cabin for the trip to Kemble, while John did his best to sell the aircraft to the Prince who of course was a qualified pilot in his own right. I then took over for the flight back to Yeovil.

We never heard any more of the requirement, and eventually the Sikorsky S 76 was chosen for the Royal Flight. Many years later the Blackhawk was chosen as the secondary aircraft for the Presidential Flight.

There were many other VIP demonstrations for Senior Service officers, including the First Sea Lord. This turned out to be Admiral Sir Benjamin Bathurst who had been an Instructor on 706 Squadron at Culdrose, who had instructed me in 1963!

CHAPTER 23

Final Days at Westlands

Having decided to stay on reaching 55 I was very happy carrying on with the production flying on Lynx and Merlin, as well as the check flights I made as a Type Rating Examiner on the Agusta 109 and Gazelle. Many other things had been going on at Westlands which did not directly affect me, but in which I was involved. The Company had won the major Apache contract to assemble 67 aircraft at Yeovil in 1996. The aircraft were supplied in kit form from Boeing so as far as Flight Test was involved it was Production testing only. However fortunately the UK wanted some major changes to the aircraft, including an engine change to the RTM 322, the same engine fitted to the Merlin, a new defensive aids suite and a new 2 inch rocket fitting. This meant there would be some development flying. The Apache was quite a complicated aircraft and the pilots for it had to undergo a conversion course at Boeings in the USA. I recruited two ex-Army test pilots, Don MaClaine and Richard Morton, who had been involved in the Army's selection process for the Apache, and were thus familiar with it. I chose not to do the conversion, as

I could not afford the time away and was very busy with the 101/Merlin development and production. I was quite happy to leave the flying to the specialist pilots and oversee the programme.

This was a major achievement by Westlands, and was helped by the firm having been taken over by GKN, a major industrial group, who had been a shareholder. The Firm now had major financial muscle behind it, and GKN were able to enjoy the profits now coming in from the Apache and Merlin programmes. The aircraft were settling into service and both saw service in Afghanistan which was very rewarding to us.

There was also a lot of production Lynx flying, in the various export versions, some new, some upgrades of the current versions. These were the Danish, German, Omani and Malaysian versions, each the same airframe but with very different avionics. It was a great pleasure to see the production aircraft being tested and then being delivered to the customer, with very few problems. It was still a great thrill for me to make the first flight of a brand new aircraft, and it was a great credit to the workforce in Yeovil and Italy that they went so smoothly.

In the early 1990's I had been sent to the Pentagon to give a presentation on the EH101 to the US Marines who manned the Presidential Flight. They flew Sikorsky S61 Sea Kings (VH3D), which had already been in service for a long time. They showed great interest, and when a competition for a replacement was announced the 101 was entered, to compete with the much smaller Sikorsky VH 92. In 2005 it was announced that the joint team of Lockheed Martin/ Agusta Westlands had been awarded the contract for the replacement aircraft for the presidential aircraft. It was a huge programme and a great victory for the European firms.

The aircraft were to be finally assembled in the USA, and nine test vehicles and pre production aircraft were ordered; construction started in 2005. First flight was in 2007, and the first five aircraft were shipped out to continue the initial testing. However the costs had escalated, mainly due to continuous changes to their requirements, and after President Obama took over in 2009 it was an obvious target for cost cutting, as well as being very unpopular politically. The whole programme was cancelled, and the Presidential flight soldiered on with their S.61. It was another five years before Sikorsky were finally awarded a contract for a version of the S92's. The 101 airframes were eventually sold to Canada for a bargain price as spares for their aircraft.

Although financially Agusta Westland were paid the massive cancelation fees the blow to the aircraft and the loss of possible future orders in the USA was severe. I was not involved in the programme as I had left by then but I would have loved to have seen the aircraft in use by the President.

As I have mentioned I decided not to retire at 55, but continued as Chief Test Pilot for another four years. I then stayed on for another year as Test Pilot and Communications Pilot. I was very happy with this arrangement, as was my successor, Don Maclaine, who had taken over as Chief Test Pilot, who was gracious enough to let me carry on. I was still happy to be flying, and not have the extra responsibilities as Chief. I was very careful not to interfere in the running of the Department.

I became very involved in the development of the Malaysian and Omani Lynx. I had recruited an ex-Navy Lynx instructor, Andy Ragget, as an instructor to accompany the aircraft on its first year in foreign service, which by now was a standard contractual requirement. In

March 2004 Andy had to come home for a period, so I was sent out to Malaysia as a replacement, for a period of four weeks.

The Malaysian Lynx were based at a heliport which was part of their main Naval base at Lumut, which is on the west coast of Malaya, about 100 miles south of Penang. The Malaysian Navy had operated Wasps for some years, so they were familiar with the concept, but the Lynx was a big step up for them. Much of the flying was Observer training under the supervision of a Royal Naval instructor who was on loan, along with a pilot. The CO of the squadron was Commander Adib, with whom I had flown back in Yeovil, accepting his aircraft. I very much enjoyed the break from flying at Yeovil, and the flying over the jungle covered mountains of Malaysia. I was also pleased to help the maintenance team to solve a long standing problem with one of the aircraft's navigation system. I noticed when airborne that the weight-on-wheels switch which indicates to the system the aircraft was airborne, was stuck in the ground position, so the navigation system wasn't activated.

I was staying at a very luxurious hotel, with a large swimming pool, and a view out over the sea. While I was in Malaysia I handed over the Chief test pilot's job to Don Maclaine, and I reverted to the normal test pilot's job after 15 years, the longest anyone had that responsibility since before the War. I had been there for the whole development and entry in to service of the EH101/Merlin, the introduction of the Apache and the improvement and development of the Lynx. During my time we had lost two aircraft, but no aircrew.

I was awarded the Derry and Richard's medal for test flying by the Guild of Airline pilots, which was presented to me by King Hussein of Jordan, at an impressive ceremony in the Guild Hall in London. I was also awarded the Alan Marsh medal by the Royal Aeronautical Society at a ceremony at their HQ in London.

In 2003 I was awarded the OBE (Order of the British Empire) for services to aviation. This was presented to me at an Investiture ceremony at Buckingham Palace by Prince Charles, who was kind enough to say he remembered flying with me. I was very proud to have my wife and two sons at the ceremony, particularly Nic, who had special permission to take one of his vital Medical School exams early so he could attend. He made it just in time! We followed it by a family lunch at the Savoy Hotel, in the company of my brother John and niece Cathy. All in all it was a very memorable and exciting day, which marked the culmination of my test flying career.

I made my last test flight for Westlands/Agusta in June 2004, just before my sixtieth birthday, appropriately it was a customer acceptance flight in an Omani Lynx with an Omani pilot. It was over Lyme bay, where I had spent so much of my flying time.

I carried on flying the communications Agusta 109's for the next five years, mainly to London but also to other UK airfields, including Heathrow. This was a very pleasant way to run down, working part time. My final helicopter flight was in June 2009, when with special permission I flew my two sons from Battersea back to Yeovil.

Facing retirement was a daunting prospect after such an active career, but it meant I could spend more time with my darling wife who has been such a support to me, and who has coped with the many separations, while bringing up a young family. I was also asked if I would consider becoming a volunteer guide at the Fleet Air Arm museum at Yeovilton. I was very happy to do this as it was a way of using my experience and I very much enjoyed sharing it with the many hundreds of visitors over the next ten years.

We also had many friends in the area, one of whom, Brian Phelan became a regular drinking partner. We came from vastly different backgrounds; he was an Irish actor and playwright, with many successful films and plays to his credit. He had been an active member of the Ban the Bomb movement, and we often smiled that while he was demonstrating in Trafalgar Square I was actually flying around carrying one!

So, with the garden, golf and five very active grand children and some flying still I kept pretty busy.

CHAPTER 24

Farnborough Air Shows

Part of the job as Chief Test Pilot was membership of the Flight Operations Committee of the Society of British Aerospace Constructors (SBAC). This was one of the many specialist committees run by SBAC, and consisted of all the Chief Test Pilots of all the firms in UK. When I first joined in 1988 the Chairman was Brian Trubshaw, famous test pilot of Concorde, who was a tremendous character, and who I held in very high regard. It was a very useful group to belong to, as we could discuss matters amongst ourselves which we were unable to even to our colleagues at work, particularly about pay and conditions. The committee formed the basis of the Flying Control Committee (FCC) for the bi-annual Air Show at Farnborough, also organised by SBAC.

When I joined Farnborough was still an RAF establishment and the Group Captain who was the CO there automatically was Chairman of the FCC. The FCC approved and supervised the flying display which ran for seven days in September, alternating every other year with the Paris show. The first five days were for trade displays with all the International Companies showing off their aircraft as best they could, and the last two days were for the public with a larger more general display, attracting crowds of 50 to 60 thousand. The week prior to the Show was Validation week when every participant had to fly their display in front of the FCC, to ensure it was safe and within the rules. The first year in which I was a member of the FCC was 1988, when there was still a lot of clear area to the north of the airfield, but as the years went on more and more of this was built on, and it became more difficult to have an unrestricted Show. The FCC monitored the show from a small converted greenhouse on top of the Control tower but when the RAF gave Farnborough up and it became a civil airport mainly dealing in Business jets a new Control Tower was built, and the old Tower demolished. The FCC were then accommodated in a purpose built Portacabin on the site of the old tower.

Obviously when I was still working it was not possible to be at Farnborough for the whole two weeks, so a roster was organised to cover the Validation and Display weeks. Inevitably most Companies tried to arrive as late as possible, so Thursday and Friday of Validation week were very busy. The Committee represented every aspect of aviation, so there was at least one expert to cover every entrant, and monitor their display. Naturally I covered the helicopters but as the years went by I became more knowledgeable on the other types, and eventually I felt confident to judge even airliners and fast jets. It was a great environment to work in, and to get to know the other Chief Test Pilots, and to meet the top pilots from all over the world.

Fortunately, we had very few problems and no accidents or incidents during my period on the committee. Our advice and rulings were invariably accepted, and we only expelled one entrant, an American fighter jet who got dangerously low over the town during the Show. Despite fierce protests from a very high level he left for home first thing next morning. Over the years there had been accidents but the regulations were now so carefully written that if the pilots obeyed them there should be no problems.

I first flew in the Show in 1966 as part of the Hermes Air Group, but then started with the Committee in 1988, and was a Member right up to 2016. When I retired as Chief test Pilot in 2004, I was asked by the Chairman of SBAC if I would take over as Chairman of the FCC for the 2004 Show. This was the year when there was a major change. The RAF had left Farnborough and this year the Show was run as a Civil Air show, under the control of the Civil Aviation Authority (CAA), and SBAC decided it would be a good time for a change of Chairman. The previous Chairman, Roger Beasley, had been in charge since 1990, when he was the last Group Captain as Superintended of flying at Farnborough. When he left the Air Force he then took over the job as a civilian until 2002. It was a major decision for me as it was a huge responsibility, very much in the public eye, and I was still working at Westlands, part time.

However I had a very helpful committee, and I spent three weeks at Farnborough, the Show week, the validation week and the week before that, making sure all was ready. Over the years Farnborough had become a base for business jets, and it became more difficult to fit in our requirements, particularly during Validation week. The customers in the jets were not used to being kept waiting! Also the area to the north of the airfield was becoming more built up, and we had to develop a special display routine to maintain a minimum height, especially for the fast jets. To monitor this we had borrowed a tracking system from the missile range in Wales, which worked very well, and we in the FCC could at all times see exactly where the aircraft was and its height. My first Show as Chairman passed without incident and I was asked if I would do it again in 2006 and 2008.

In 2009 SBAC became ADS and responsibility for the Air Show was transferred to a new Company, Farnborough International Ltd (FI). The Show was moved to July.

I had many highlights of the Show, but there were some very memorable moments. Seeing the big airliners close up, especially the Airbus 380 on its first appearance was always impressive. In the early 90's Russia had a large presence and its fast jets gave a unique display. The Red Arrows were always very impressive, but one year they had a bird strike, and eventually the new rules limited their display to a flypast. I acted as Chairman again in 2008, but declined after that. I had supervised three safe and successful displays, and didn't want to push my luck! John Turner who had been Chief test Pilot at British Aerospace at Warton, who had acted as my Deputy, took over as Chairman, and I acted as Deputy for 2010 and 2012. We had a very good working relationship which continued on to Bahrain.

As the years went by it became more and more difficult to hold an Air Show at Farnborough. In the 50's and 60's Farnborough was the biggest Show in the world, was limited to British aircraft only, and had a large Service input. Frequently it was the first appearance of a new type, and attracted huge crowds. As the UK industry declined foreign aircraft were permitted, and the British Service input became much more limited. When it became a civil show, it was more restricted and the Hunter crash at the Shoreham show made the CAA even more aware of their responsibilities, and the whole necessity for Air Shows was questioned. The civil rules and regulations were revised and rewritten when it was realised the rules protected the paying audience, at the expense of the audience outside. This had an immediate effect on the Farnborough Show, and the rules had to be carefully revised. The Farnborough Air Show was provided to allow manufacturers to demonstrate the capabilities of their product, but such is the complexity and cost of modern aircraft that choosing a new type is only done after a long and careful assessment, including flying, at the manufacturers, rather than seeing a display at Farnborough.

The last Show in which I was involved was 2016, when I was a part time member of the FCC. It had been difficult to get enough aircraft for a reasonable Show, particularly for the public days, and inevitably after the Show was cancelled in 2020, the public days were permanently cancelled from 2022 onwards. The five Trade days remained.

CHAPTER 25

❋

Bahrain Air Shows

In 2009 the Kingdom of Bahrain decided they wished to hold their own Aerospace Exhibition and Flying display, following the pattern of Dubai, who had been holding their own Show for several years. Nothing happens in Bahrain without Royal approval, and one of the King's two sons was given the Air show to organise, and the other son given the Grand Prix! As they had no experience in this field, it was decided to sub contract the whole Show to Farnborough International to organise and run on the same lines as the Farnborough Show. This was a major success for FI, but they needed a Flying Display Director. I had just retired as FDD for the 2008 show, and was asked by the Chairman of FI if I would consider taking on the job. The fee was very attractive, and the challenge of setting up a new show from scratch was also attractive. I decided to accept, and thus became the flying Display Director for the 2010, 2012 and 2014 shows.

The Show was planned for three days in January, the coolest time of year, and would be held at the Sakhir Air force base, the home of the Royal Flight. There was a huge hangar there, large enough to house two Boeing 747's! There was one long runway, and very little traffic, ideal for an Air Show. I needed the experience of another FCC member, and Vic Lockwood volunteered. Vic had been the Chief Test Pilot of Flight Refuelling, and we had worked together on several Shows, and had become firm friends. This was the start of many trips to Bahrain on Gulfair. Our first visit to Sakhir showed how much work was required before it was ready for the show. The permanent chalets had not been built, and the car parks were a pile of rubble. The senior Bahraini in charge was the head of the Bahraini Air Force, and it soon became obvious he was not too keen on the job. In fact he only did it for the first show in 2010, and after that it became the responsibility of the head of the Bahraini CAA.

A colonel in the Bahraini Air Force, an F16 pilot, was attached to the FCC, and soon proved invaluable with his local contacts. Also attached was a Senior Pilot of the Royal Flight, who was eventually to be based at Sakhir, but in 2010 were still based at the International Airport. The Show was quite modest by Farnborough standards but there were single jet displays by Boeing in an F16, by the French in a Raphale, by the US Navy in an F18 and by the Russians in a Sukhoi 21. There were team displays by the French, by the UAE and by the Saudis in their Green Arrows, a direct copy of the Red Arrows. As aviation is tightly controlled in Bahrain there was no conflict with other traffic, and the Show ran very smoothly. There was no public day as such, but there was a public area for 5000 people which was rapidly sold out. This area was some way from the display centre which resulted in some criticism.

The Show was considered a great success and I was asked to repeat it in 2012. This Show followed the same pattern, with several formation displays with the major addition of the Knights Russian team in their large Su. 27's, who were rarely seen ouside Russia. As we knew very little about them we were very cautious until we saw their first show, when it was obvious they were extremely professional with an exceptional Show. There were several solo fast jets each trying to demonstrate their capabilities to potential customers, including the British Typhoon.

The 2014 Show was increased again with a similar programme, with the Russian knights again. This time they had an unexpected addition, the firing of flares from the aircraft while in a vertical climb. While very impressive unfortunately each flare had a metal cap, which were scattered over the airfield, a real hazard to other aircraft. When I informed the Russian General in charge that I could not permit this he was most put out, but eventually had to accept it.

The Shows had grown in size each time, and after three safe and successful shows I thought it was time for someone else to take over. Yet again John Turner stepped in for the 2016 Show, but I stayed on as Deputy to help with the handover. This Show was marked by the non-appearance of the Russian Knights.

The 2018 Show was moved to November to better alternate with the Dubai Show, and had much the same content, this time with the Russian formation team again. It would seem that the Show we started in 2010 has now become part of the International Display programme, and Bahrain is very proud of that.

CHAPTER 26

Retirement and Back to Fixed Wing

I was fortunate to be able to carry on test flying at Agusta/ Westlands until I was 60, and then carry on as Communications pilot for another five years. However I was starting to realise that after flying for over forty years I was going to miss it very much. Fortunately for me a solution appeared.

A friend and colleague, Brian Main, who had been one of the Chief Designers for the EH 101/Merlin, was also coming up to retirement, and had plans to build a light kit aircraft in his garage. Brian was a meticulous engineer, and asked me if I would come in with him on the project financially, and then fly the aircraft when it was built. This was a perfect solution for me, and I had absolute faith in Brian's ability to construct an aircraft which was safe.

The aircraft he chose, the Van RV9A, is from a range of kit aircraft produced by the Van aircraft company in the USA designed for the home builder. It is a low wing two seater, non aerobatic, optimised for long distance cruising. It has a top speed of140 knots, a stalling speed of about 40 knots, and an endurance of about five hours. The kit comes in sections, the first one the tail plane and rudder, then the wings and finally the fuselage. It took Brian more than two years of fairly continuous effort, but we finished up with a superb little red and white aircraft, with a very reliable Lycoming engine.

There wasn't anything I could do to help during construction, but I was busy obtaining my Private Pilot's Licence (PPL). I did it at the Devon flying school at Dunkeswell, an ex-WW 2 airfield near Honiton. Although it was more than 40 years since I had flown a fixed wing aircraft (a Chipmunk at ETPS) I was confident it would only take a couple of trips to be safe to fly solo again. My very experienced instructor, Gill Rudham, warned me it it might take longer, and she was absolutely right! It took almost seven hours before she thought I was safe to go solo. That was all in a club Cessna, and having obtained my National Private Pilot's Licence, I did my conversion to our own aircraft, G-CCGU, and my first flight in it was on 4th November 2004. The aircraft was a delight to fly, and gave me much pleasure for the next thirteen years.

While he was building it Brian also gained his PPL, and we were joined by a third member, Andy Strachan, one of my successors at Agusta/Westlands. I was never brave enough to venture very far by myself, but with Brian I went to the Isle of Wight, to Cornwall and one trip abroad to Cherbourg for lunch. Most of my flying was for General Handling to maintain my currency. We kept the aircraft at Dunkeswell where it had been finally assembled, but eventually moved it to Henstridge, another WW2 airfield only three miles from my home, which was very convenient.

However I had noticed for some time my left hand was getting weaker, and starting to tremor. When consulting a Neurologist he diagnosed Parkinson's disease and a muscular condition. There is no cure for either of these, but they can be kept in check by medication. It was though the end of my flying after over fifty years, and over eight thousand hours. I had had some narrow escapes, and lost a number of friends and colleagues, but had vastly enjoyed the majority of it, and helped the development of a helicopter which has already saved hundreds of lives, which is some achievement.

When the Covid Pandemic broke out, and we were constrained to our homes for weeks on end, it was the ideal time to write my memoirs, helped by my log books. It has taken over two years of single figure typing, but it has brought back to me the memories of a very busy career, and I am very grateful to all the engineers and technicians who ensured I finished my career with the same number of landings as takeoffs.

Brush with Fame

It was in April 1994, when I was working as Chief Test Pilot at Westland Helicopters, that we had an unusual request from 10 Downing Street. We were developing the new large EH 101 helicopter, one version of which was a 30 seat passenger/VIP variant. The Prime Minister at the time, John Major, was aware of our desire to sell the aircraft, and that any exposure would be valuable. We were thus asked if we could provide the aircraft to ferry him and his guest, Chancellor Kohl of Germany, from Northolt airport to Chequers for lunch, and then back to central London.

I was somewhat nervous about this, as shortly before, on what was a demonstration flight from Northolt, in a similar prototype, for the Dutch Minister of Defence we had had a very unfortunate incident. The large flotation bag, which is normally tucked away inside the aircraft, chose that moment to come loose in a very dramatic manner. Unfortunately, it was the bag that was directly below the window where the Minister was sitting. He was very polite about it, but was obviously a bit shaken, so the flight was cut short, and they showed no further interest in the aircraft!

Sure, that this could not happen again, we were delighted to do this VVIP flight, but there was a large problem. The aircraft was a prototype, full of instrumentation, and in no way suitable for VIP transport. It was decided we could remove some instrumentation, and fit some temporary passenger seats. However, these were rather narrow, and the Chancellor was a very large gentleman! The protocol officer from the German Embassy went to great pains to emphasise that we should not make any obvious measures to accommodate the Chancellor, such as one large seatbelt from one side of the seat to another, which was one idea. Another was one large "club class" seat, which would have made it very obvious. Just as were running out of ideas, it transpired that the Chancellor's interpreter was a very slight girl, and that there would be room on same seat for both of them. The other normal sized passengers (the PM and his team) were easily accommodated.

Everything then depended on the weather, as we had to be able to fly visually from Northolt to Chequers. As usual, on the morning in question, the weather at Northolt was marginal, but was forecast to clear by the time of the flight. An early decision, which was mine alone, had to be made, as alternative road transport would have had to be provided. If they had to make the journey by car, it would have cut short the visit to Chequers, if not cancelled it, and of course would not show the aircraft in a very good light. No pressure then!

I decided to risk it, and flew up to Northolt. To my dismay, much of the flight was in cloud, there seemed no sign of the forecast clearance and we had to make an instrument approach in to Northolt. We then had a short wait for the Chancellor's aircraft to arrive, during which, to my enormous relief, the weather cleared sufficiently.

We also had to ensure that the airstair door was suitable for Mr. Major, as on his previous flight in the military version, with a different door with a much higher first step, he had refused to get in until we had shut down the aircraft completely. He has difficulty with steps, due to an old knee injury. This time there was no problem.

The VIP's arrived, and embarked, with the Chancellor not looking too impressed with the very basic interior of the prototype helicopter. However, the PM did a great sales job, explaining the situation, as he had had a demonstration flight some months previously. The flight to Chequers went perfectly, only 15 minutes, saving them a lengthy car journey.

We landed on the immaculate lawn at Chequers and the VIP's disembarked for lunch. To our surprise we were also shown into Chequers, where at the door we were carefully, but politely separated. We aircrew were ushered into the Senior Staff quarters and had a delicious lunch. The engineers were shown into the chauffeurs' room!

After lunch, while waiting for the passengers, we found our 14 ton helicopter had sunk in to the lawn up to the wheel rims. On landing the bottom of the airstair door was four inches above the surface, but it was now resting on the ground! Fortunately, nobody else noticed this.

The passengers re-embarked, in a much happier state of mind. They were rather late back from lunch, but to speed things up on the return trip, the PM suggested that all the passengers pedalled harder! Maybe this did not translate well, as there was little German reaction. On taking off we left four very large holes in the immaculate Chequers lawn. We flew them back to London in glorious weather. With our VIP status we were permitted to fly directly across central London, a most unusual privilege. We landed in Wellington Barracks, enormously impressing the large crowd of tourists.

We had a very nice thank you note from Number 10, but unfortunately, we never did sell any civil variant of the EH101, but we did sell several VVIP versions.

※

Night Fright

Towards the end 1969 I was the Flight Commander of a Wasp Flight based on an Anti-submarine frigate, HMS Yarmouth. We were attached to the Far East Fleet (yes, we had one in those days), and we were exercising in the South China sea to the east of Malaysia. There was a standing requirement to fly at least 15 hours a month, five of which had to be at night. With the ship's programme this was sometimes difficult to achieve so I had planned an hour's flight practicing weapon drops controlled by radar from the ship. This was the Wasp's primary role, dropping a homing torpedo on a submarine detected by another source, so we practised a lot, using other surface targets. The ship's radar was controlled by the Helicopter Control Officer (HCO) via a UHF radio link, which was obviously vital. Not least for getting back to the ship, and in bad weather making a radar controlled approach. The radio link was so vital the Wasp had two radios, one main, and one emergency with only two frequencies, one of which was the international distress frequency 243.0. We always checked this with the ship before takeoff.

On this particular night the weather was rather challenging, solid cloud cover at about 1000 feet, absolutely flat calm with the sea like a black mirror. There was no horizon, and it was absolutely impossible to tell up from down, flight solidly on instruments from take-off to landing.

The standard operating height for the Wasp was 400 feet, which we accepted at the time, but in retrospect fills me with horror. It had a small highly loaded rotor, so the rate of descent in autorotation was very fast. In the event of engine failure, one had to very rapidly enter autorotation, with only a few seconds before you hit the sea, in which time you had to flare and turn into wind, at night of course all on instruments! Engine failure was a distinct possibility, of the 96 Wasps built 24 were lost, many of them with engine failure.

So having checked the radios with the HCO (a particular friend of mine) I launched off into the darkness, all by myself. I was used to flying at night but this absolute blackness was quite disorientating. I was directed towards the first target, some miles away. I overflew the target, a small native fishing vessel, and was directed towards another. After a while I had had no further directions, and when I called there was no reply. I was starting to get worried by now, as I knew there were several islands in the area with mountains up to 3400 feet, and I couldn't see anything at all. One of them, Pulau Tioman, is now an exotic holiday resort but at the time was a near deserted tropical island which had been used in the film South Pacific. As the ship's radar was my only way of knowing where these were I was rather poorly placed at 400 feet.

If in doubt climb to safe altitude, so I shot up through the cloud to 4000 feet. This should also have increased my chances of contacting the ship, but still no reply to my increasingly frantic calls. I changed to the standby radio in case the problem was at my end, but still no joy. The possibility now emerged of the ship having a radio failure, which should never happen as it had several UHF radios. Even so this contingency had been thought of, and the Royal Navy had a procedure for dealing with it (as it does for everything). The HCO had to leg it from the Ops room to the Bridge roof carrying a portable battery powered radio, preset to the guard frequency. Still I had no contact even on Guard. By this time I was getting a bit short of fuel. The Wasp had a limited endurance of about 1 hour 20 minutes, and I had been airborne for about 40 minutes. I turned back towards where I thought the ship might be. Like most Wasp pilots I had been trying to keep a mental plot of my and the ship's position, but by now it had become hopelessly confused.

By now I was beginning to get really worried. I had no land diversion, there was no national emergency frequencies to help, as there is in UK, and I had absolutely no idea where the ship was. However, by a fortunate coincidence, another RN frigate, HMS Galatea, had also been exercising with its Wasp, some miles to the south of us and had heard my calls on guard, just before they shutdown having finished their own flying. At last, a friendly voice! I explained the problem, and started to home towards them, using the very basic UHF homing device on the Wasp. Meanwhile they were attempting to contact my ship and were rapidly stowing their Wasp so I could land and refuel. They eventually saw my transponder and cleared me back down to 400 feet. After a radar approach I landed on Galatea, and refuelled. I was never so grateful to see those few little deck lights in the pitch black! After some words of encouragement from my fellow Flight Commander on Galatea (another good mate) and the confirmation of my ship's position, I took off and made my way back, about 30 miles to meet my ship thundering towards me.

So what had happened? Shortly after I got airborne the ship had suffered a total electrical failure, another of these occurrences which should never happen, and it took quite a while to get things back on line, including all the radios and radar. Meanwhile I had cheerfully disappeared over the horizon. And the standby portable? Of course it only had a short range. When we had previously used it I had been close to the ship.

One good thing came out of it, the Weapons Electrical officer bought me a beer once I got back!

APPENDIX 3

Royal Naval Reserve Air Branch

In 1980, not long after I left the Navy, someone in the Service had the bright idea of reforming the Reserve Air Branch. It had last been in existence in the 1950's when special Squadrons were formed of recently retired pilots who maintained their currency by flying at weekends. They were thus readily available in an emergency. The Branch was disbanded in the 1957.

The new plan was again to recruit air crew who had just left, and attach them to front line Squadrons for a fortnight every year for refresher training. Thus there would be a pool of aircrew who would require a minimal amount of training to be operationally ready. Most of them were in aviation jobs and most of the employers supported the scheme, and like Westlands, allowed an extra weeks leave. They joined the Squadrons they had recently left, in my case 815 at Yeovilton, flying Lynx. My first training fortnight was at the end of December 1980, and was a very useful mixture of General Flying practice, instrument flying and operational flying, none of which I could carry out at

Westlands. When the Branch first formed it was 30 strong, all pilots or Observers.

Then followed a two week period every year, which was very useful for me professionally, and also for me to check on the Navy's view of Westlands, as they were our prime customer.

815 Squadron moved to Portland, and I managed the fortnightly training every year from 1982 to 1989, although it was getting more difficult to spare the time from Westlands, as by this time I was the Chief Test Pilot. In 1990 I was very pleased to be promoted to Commander, and to be made head of the Branch, a job which lasted three years. This meant I was no longer required to carry out the fortnightly training, but spend separate days on administration, and supervising the annual training weekend and Dinner. This meant I had to host the senior guest, who was often the First Sea Lord!

The Air branch has been a huge success, and is now more than 300 strong, and now includes ratings and technical personnel as well as Aircrew.

The highlight for me was in 1989 when one of my guests for dinner was Captain Jock Lowe, the senior training Captain for the British Airways Concorde fleet. British Airways had always been a strong supporter of the Branch, and he had been invited as a way of thanks. We were talking about Concorde, and he asked me if I would like a trip! Of course I was thrilled, and shortly after a ticket arrived for a day trip to New York. The take off from Heathrow was at 1000, and the flight lasted two and a half hours, just time to have a delicious lunch. After waiting at JFK airport I boarded for the return flight, this time with Jock at the controls. After dinner he invited me up to cockpit, where I remained until after landing. It was an unforgettable day.

I had to leave the Branch at the end of my three year spell as Head. I was sorry to leave after 30 years service with the Royal Navy, but I had plenty to keep me busy at Westlands.